Nordic Film Classics
METTE HJORT and PETER SCHEPELERN, *Series Editors*

NORDIC FILM CLASSICS

The Nordic Film Classics series offers in-depth studies of key films by Danish, Finnish, Icelandic, Norwegian, and Swedish directors. Written by emerging as well as established film scholars, and where possible in conversation with relevant film practitioners, these books help to shed light on the ways in which the Nordic nations and region have contributed to the art of film.

Ingmar Bergman's "The Silence": Pictures in the Typewriter, Writings on the Screen by Maaret Koskinen

Dagur Kari's "Nói the Albino" by Björn Norðfjörð

Lone Scherfig's "Italian for Beginners" by Mette Hjort

Lukas Moodysson's "Show Me Love" by Anna Westerståhl Stenport

Lukas Moodysson's

Show Me Love

Anna Westerståhl Stenport

UNIVERSITY OF WASHINGTON PRESS
Seattle

MUSEUM TUSCULANUM PRESS
Copenhagen

This book was made possible by the generous support of the Campus Research Board of the University of Illinois at Urbana-Champaign.

Copyright © 2012 by the University of Washington Press
Printed in the United States of America
Design by Thomas Eykemans
16 15 14 13 12 17   5 4 3 2 1

All rights reserved. No part of this publication may be reproduced or transmitted in any form or by any means, electronic or mechanical, including photocopy, recording, or any information storage or retrieval system, without permission in writing from the publisher.

Published in the United States by
UNIVERSITY OF WASHINGTON PRESS
PO Box 50096, Seattle, WA 98145, USA
www.washington.edu/uwpress

Published in Europe by
MUSEUM TUSCULANUM PRESS
University of Copenhagen
126 Njalsgade, DK-2300 Copenhagen S, Denmark
www.mtp.dk
978 87 635 3881 7

LIBRARY OF CONGRESS CATALOGING-IN-PUBLICATION DATA
Stenport, Anna Westerståhl.
Lukas Moodysson's Show me love / Anna Westerståhl Stenport.
    p. cm.
Includes bibliographical references and index. Includes filmography.
ISBN 978-0-295-99180-1 (pbk. : alk. paper)
1. Show me love (Motion picture) 2. Moodysson, Lukas, 1969– Criticism and interpretation. I. Title.
PN1997.S4782S74 2012   791.43'72—dc23   2011043712

The paper used in this publication is acid-free and 90 percent recycled from at least 50 percent post-consumer waste. It meets the minimum requirements of American National Standard for Information Sciences—Permanence of Paper for Printed Library Materials, ANSI Z39.48–1984.

Contents

Acknowledgments	vii
1. MOODYSSON'S CONTEXTS	3
2. THE AMBIVALENCE OF *SHOW ME LOVE*	28
3. THE GEOGRAPHY OF *SHOW ME LOVE*	86
4. MOODYSSON'S CONTINUATION	123
Festival Screenings and Awards	138
Notes	142
Bibliography	179
Filmography	196
Index	201

Acknowledgments

Writing this book took me on journeys to unexpected places and led me to many wonderful people who graciously shared their time, knowledge, and resources with me. I am truly grateful to each and every one and to the funding agencies that made this journey and these meetings possible. Many practitioners in the Swedish and Nordic film industry have provided invaluable input—their participation has been an integral part of this project since its inception, as the bibliographic record of individuals interviewed at the end of the book shows. I am grateful to Lars Jönsson, Charlotta Denward, Bengt Toll, Mikael Timm, Ola Törjas, Rasmus Thord, Marit Kapla, Louise Martin, Ulrika Nisell, Tomas Eskilsson, Katarina Krave, Charlotte Appelgren, Jeanette Gentele, Ulf Brantås, and Josefin Åsberg. I also wish to thank director Lukas Moodysson for sharing his time so generously with me.

Many members of the academic community in North America and Scandinavia have provided supportive and productive criticism at different stages of the project. Thank you Andy Nestingen, Maaret Koskinen, Yvonne Leffler, Mariah Larsson, Olle Hedling,

Jenny Björklund, Per Assmo, Roger Blomgren, Mikael Jonasson, Sarah Projansky, Bob Pahre, Anke Pinkert, Brett Ashley Kaplan, Jon Ebel, Mark Sandberg, Linda Rugg, and, of course, the Urbana Friday afternoon writing group: Ericka Beckman, Ellen Moodie, and Yasemin Yildiz. For helpful discussions and assistance with bibliographic matters, formatting, and copyediting, I thank research assistants Kurt Hollender, Lawrence Smith, Paul Hartley, and Jon Sherman. I also wish to thank Nordic Film Classics series editors Mette Hjort and Peter Schepelern for their invitation to contribute to the series and their, as well as that of an anonymous reviewer's, extraordinarily helpful feedback. Working with the University of Washington Press staff and senior acquisitions editor Jacquie Ettinger has been a wonderful experience.

Funding to initiate and complete this book and related research projects has been generously awarded from the following sources: University of Illinois Research Board, University of Illinois European Union Center, University of Illinois Center for International Business Education and Research, the American Scandinavian Foundation, the Barbro Osher Pro Suecia Foundation, the Swedish Institute, Helge Ax:son Johnson Foundation, and Åke Wiberg Foundation. Sections of chapters 1 and 3 first appeared in an essay titled "Local and Global: Lukas Moodysson and Swedish Film," published in *Swedish Film: An Introduction and a Reader*, eds. Mariah Larsson and Anders Marklund (Nordic Academic Press, 2011: 325–333), and are reprinted with permission here.

This book could not have been completed without the support of a number of people close to my heart who have helped in numerous ways, big and small, while I traveled to Sweden for interviews and to access material, and then returned home to write. Members of the Stenport and Westerståhl families have done what they do so well:

show unwavering support; Olof and Ingegerd, in particular—thank you! This book is for my mother, and it comes with more gratitude than is possible to imagine.

Lukas Moodysson's *Show Me Love*

1
Moodysson's Contexts

In the mid-1990s, Lukas Moodysson (b. 1969) was best known, if at all, in his home country Sweden as an obscure poetic prodigy in the modernist tradition, having published his first collection of poems with a prestigious publisher at age seventeen. His breakthrough debut feature as director and scriptwriter, *Show Me Love* (*Fucking Åmål*, 1998), made him a household name overnight. This film was enthusiastically received in all major media outlets, seen by nearly 900,000 viewers in Sweden, and subsequently received four *Guldbaggar*—the Swedish equivalent of Oscars at the Academy Awards—including best film, best director, best screenplay, and best actors (Alexandra Dahlström and Rebecca Liljeberg). In Sweden, *Show Me Love* was soon thereafter considered a youth film classic, while international reception saw it as related to the New Queer Cinema wave of the early 1990s.[1] This coming-of-age and coming-out film about two young women in a stiflingly oppressive small town indeed became a favorite at international gay and lesbian film festivals, though Swedish reception initially downplayed its queer elements. *Show Me Love* was selected as Sweden's film for the Academy

Awards, won the Teddy Award at the Berlin Film Festival in 1999, and was subsequently screened all over the world, at film festivals as well as in regular distribution.

Show Me Love, shot on a limited budget in small-town Trollhättan with largely amateur and young actors, was quickly recognized as a watershed mark in Swedish film history. Ingmar Bergman called Moodysson "a master" and *Show Me Love* "a masterpiece," while distinguished film scholar Leif Furhammar labeled it as a film that ignited a "depressed" Swedish film industry of the mid-1990s with "hope and enthusiasm."[2] Well-known film director Stefan Jarl later declared Moodysson "a genius," and journalist Jannike Åhlund describes a perception of Moodysson at the time of *Show Me Love*'s release as "Swedish film's savior."[3] International critics tend to relate Moodysson to his famous predecessor, positioning him as "the most celebrated Swedish film director after Ingmar Bergman."[4]

Show Me Love's extraordinary success gave Moodysson a stable platform from which to subsequently experiment with a range of topics, approaches, styles, and cinematic forms. Moodysson has released five additional feature films: *Together* (*Tillsammans*, 2000); *Lilya 4-ever* (*Lilja 4-ever*, 2002); *A Hole in My Heart* (*Ett hål i mitt hjärta*, 2005); *Container* (2006); and *Mammoth* (*Mammut*, 2009). Having just finished *Show Me Love*, Moodysson also cowrote the script to an acclaimed television mini-series, *The New Country* (*Det nya landet*, 2000), with Peter Birro, subsequently released as a feature film with the same title. After *Lilya 4-ever*, he codirected a controversial documentary, *The Kids They Sentenced* (*Terrorister: En film om dom dömda*, 2003; with Stefan Jarl). Moodysson has also continued writing poetry and narrative prose,[5] and has further made forays into experimental photography. Though divergent in scope, there is one unifying trope of his films: children and adolescents feature prominently, often as vehicles of critical perspicuity, affective connection, and audience identification. In *Show Me Love*, Elin and Agnes' teenage romance challenges social norms and foregrounds repressive aspects of conventional Swedish small-town life. In *Together*, 13-year-old Eva (Emma Samuelsson) declares her opinion that, as they are self-absorbed and careless, all "adults are idiots"; and in *Container*'s art film inspired monologue, we sense that a small child has been trapped in an adult body. Moodysson has affirmed in numerous interviews that this is, indeed, a privileged perspective for him: "I think I am trying to find the childish perspective in myself the whole time as a writer. When people criticize me for being childish or naïve . . . to me that is just a compliment because I am just trying to find that perspective or that point of view."[6] Moodysson's comments about his interest in conveying a child's point of view implicitly illustrate a primary concern in his oeuvre: an explicit interest in authenticity. Moodysson's interest in authenticity is further developed in two recent prose narratives, one framed as semi-autobiographical, *Döden & Co* (Death and Company, 2011); another as a direct biographical report from the author's own life, *En vacker sjuk plats* (A Beautiful Sick Place, 2012).[7] The perspective of youth and children so often evoked in his films connotes an investment in authenticity as well as innocence.

Authenticity, Ambivalence, Aesthetics

Plot and characterization in most of Moodysson's films appear to support a notion that the films engage with what can be broadly construed as contemporary reality; like *Show Me Love*, most films tend to focus on everyday situations, locations, and practices, with dialogue scripted in colloquial language. The director himself has repeatedly stated that he wants to make films that appear authentic, that matter, that have a social significance, and that can have an impact in the world. "Authenticity" is a notoriously complex term, however, and the kind of cinematic authenticity of interest to Moodysson appears to draw most explicitly on a social realist tradition. British directors Mike Leigh and Ken Loach; Russian Andrei Tarkovsky; Americans Martin Scorsese and John Cassavetes; and Swedes Bo Widerberg, Roy Andersson, and Stefan Jarl are all sources of inspiration for him, as he himself regularly recounts. These directors establish clear, affective, and emotional points of connection with an audience. Moodysson carries this legacy through his films and implements it via meticulous casting, scripting dialogue that reflects contemporary circumstances and linguistic expressions, forgoing extensive rehearsal, employing a cinematic aesthetic that draws on documentary techniques (including the limited manipulation of lighting, use of filters, or implementation of other visual effects), incorporating expressive music (particularly pop music, which is made to correlate with themes and characterization), and advocating for extremely detailed production design (locations—domestic interiors in particular—are highly significant in all of his films). Cast, crew, and other personnel who have worked with Moodysson (many of whom are interviewed in this book) have repeatedly pointed to the author's professed dedication to authenticity, whether in dialogue, casting, direction, or production design.

Moodysson's self-professed interest in authenticity also involves other aspects of his filmmaking. He describes his personality as "ambivalent" and as looking for the middle ground, searching for compromises rather than extreme positions.[8] Strong-willed as a director and cinematic practitioner, he himself sees a connection between ambivalence and authenticity as central to his practice and oeuvre. This is, he says, "why I think I am so good at writing dialogue; I can argue and present both sides of everything."[9] Moodysson's use of "ambivalent" to describe himself as being able to see two sides of an issue complements a more common use of the term in English. Ambivalence is usually understood as holding contradictory attitudes or feelings about any given issue. This definition of ambivalence in fact holds true for most of Moodysson's work as well. Assessing his own legacy, Moodysson sees himself both as an explicitly "aggressive" and "political filmmaker," yet one who is also "kind and religious."[10]

From this perspective, Moodysson's films capture social moments and portray contemporary complexity. Critics have generally tended to see Moodysson's interest in authenticity located on a personal and narrative level. He "puts story-telling and the personal statement in front of [ahead of] form" and "human beings interest him more than aesthetics."[11] Yet, critical to Moodysson's oeuvre is that his films are both products of their time—always in explicit engagement with contemporary or recent popular culture—and products of aesthetic and affective experimentation. His films depend on significant and divergent formal and structural experimentation.

Moodysson's films combine a socially and emotionally invested impetus with cinematic aesthetic experimentation, whether in the form of reverse film stock in *Show Me Love*,[12] a production-design immersion experiment in *Together*, reality-TV inspired digital video in *A Hole in My Heart*, or a postmodernist disconnect between image and soundtracks in *Container*. Even *Mammoth*'s explicit use of wide-screen cinemascope aspect ratio is part of a continuing experimentation that attempts to portray human depravity against visually stunning backgrounds. Moodysson's films have continuously experimented with form—whether in terms of camera work, technology, production design, direction, editing, or soundtrack.

Part of Moodysson's aesthetic, established in *Show Me Love* and subsequently expanded, is to allow cinematic form and production practices to shape and contribute to the social and affective outcome of each individual film. Yet, all of Moodysson's films remain emotionally, socially, and politically ambivalent, and often problematically so. Though some aspects of all his films can appear didactic or even moralizing, rarely can a clear synthesis or simplistic message be derived from them. This cinematic trajectory was established in *Show Me Love* and continues through Moodysson's career. This book contextualizes this ambivalence as part of a search for authenticity and draws out its implications along a number of lines.

Despite Moodysson's significance for Swedish and European film during the last decade and a half, relatively little has been written about this director and his films—especially for an international audience. This book presents Moodysson's *Show Me Love* to a broad range of readers, international as well as Swedish. It follows the assumption that films are complex cultural products and that filmmaking is a comprehensive collective process. It thereby emphasizes practice-based aspects of filmmaking, including efforts involved not only in funding, producing, and distributing a film but also in collective responses to the finished product, including media and scholarly reception, awards, and other aspects of making a legacy. Information in this book is culled from a large number of interviews with Moodysson and people who are closely associated with him and have been influential in his cinematic oeuvre. Other sources include interviews with Swedish and international film scholars and journalists,[13] as well as material from general as well as academic publications.

I take seriously Moodysson's interest in authenticity as reflective not only of his agency as a practitioner of cinematic arts but also of concerns in Swedish and European film industries during the decades flanking the turn of the millennium. This investigation, which bridges inquiry into production practices with close readings of film sequences, focuses on two unifying themes of Moodysson's oeuvre. Both are at the forefront of *Show Me Love* and establish a foundation for Moodysson's subsequent work. The first involves representations of sexuality and gender, particularly as ambivalently perceived and performed by adolescents and young adults. The second involves attention to spatiality as an authentic conveyor of social and affective ambivalence. The spatial elements include filming location (on-site, place substitutions, or in studio) and production design (scenography, sets, and props). Funding and industry parameters also have a spatial quality, as they have transformed the geography of where and how films are made in Sweden and Europe in the twenty-first century. Moodysson's films have been instrumental in shaping contemporary Swedish film history in both respects.

The three chapters of this book explore how Moodysson's films offer unique ways for understanding the role and function of contemporary cinema by linking place and gender, sexuality and space. In this first chapter, I outline Moodysson's background and his development as a filmmaker. I discuss key aspects of his practice as a scriptwriter and director, and indicate the people and institutions that have been crucial for his career as a whole. I also include brief references to film history and relevant cultural context. The second chapter is a focused study of *Show Me Love*. It addresses conditions of production, media reception, and thematic and aesthetic analyses. In particular, it investigates this film's representations of gender and sexuality as fluid, uncertain, constructed, and ambivalent. Chapter three involves a discussion of *Show Me Love*'s geography in terms of international reception, its cinematic landscape, and the functions of location and local production conditions, and outlines this film's significance for Swedish and European film industries.

A Filmmaker by Accident?

Moodysson grew up in the small town of Åkarp outside Malmö in southern Sweden, the son of divorced parents, a librarian and an engineer. He has two older sisters. He describes growing up in a "normal" environment, in "a very normal small town, in very normal surroundings," with parents and a stepfather who were supportive but not part of a cultural or political establishment, yet who helped instill in him a sense that "I was special in some way and very normal as well."[14] Atypically, Moodysson chose to drop out of high school in order to write poetry. He was remarkably productive, allying himself with an impressive press to publish four poetry collections and one novel by age 21, and supporting himself in the meantime by tending bars and working odd jobs.[15] He was a part of the poetry collective *Malmöligan* (the Malmö collective), which staged performance readings and public events in an avant-gardist tradition. He moved to Stockholm to start film school in 1992 and upon graduation in 1995 left the capital to settle for a period outside the small town of Örebro and later in another small town, Kungälv, near Sweden's second-largest city, Göteborg. He returned to live in Malmö at the time of completing *Show Me Love*. He is married to Coco Moodysson, a visual artist and writer, with whom he has three children. Moodysson has declared himself as politically to the left of Sweden's Social Democratic Party and as a Christian—the latter an unusual public stance in contemporary secularized Sweden—but states that he does not participate in organized religious activities.

Moodysson keeps a low public profile, preferring relative anonymity in his hometown Malmö and at his family's summerhouse in the southern province Småland to media appearances. Earlier in his career he was known as a rebel poet and as an outspoken, though not always consistent, social critic. At the red-carpet *Guldbagge* Award Ceremony in 1999 for *Show Me Love*, for example, Moodysson lectured the glitzy audience (and television viewers at home) on the merits of vegetarianism and socialism, even proclaiming he did not want his *Guldbagge* because of the shallow commercialism of the award event. These statements (and his giving the audience the finger) gave him a public image as a radical and moralizing outsider. Later examples include his public stance against the harsh sentencing of youth participants in anti-EU and anti-US rallies in Göteborg in 2001 and against human trafficking and prostitution. With the exception of planned media appearances and press conferences, his current low profile has positioned him as somewhat marginal in contemporary Swedish public life. Agreeing to be interviewed for this book, as well as authorizing the participation of many long-term collaborators, suggests a significant interest in actively shaping his legacy and in wanting to expand on a concept already established as central to Moodysson's self-presentation: to contribute to an authentic portrayal of his career as a filmmaker.

Moodysson has indicated in a number of interviews that turning to film as a mode of expression was half-accidental: "My interest in movies came . . . out of being very bored with my life. . . . For some reason, I don't really know why, I just started to make films."[16] Even for a published and critically acclaimed poet, it was no small feat to be accepted into Sweden's most prestigious film education program at Stockholm's Dramatiska Institutet on his first attempt. "I am not quite sure why they let me into the program," he says with some bewilderment. "I was never a film buff and I had no experience writing scripts, making film, or working with actors. I hardly knew film was edited. During the mock-directing session, I remember myself as obstinate, and as refusing to take suggestions. Maybe that's what the committee liked."[17] At Dramatiska Institutet, other students wanted to "make dark and difficult films," Moodysson continues, "but I was used to a different kind of life," and he wanted to make different kinds of films.[18] Moodysson recognizes the influence of mainstream American cinema on his early films: "I tried finding those simple, straightforward communicative methods of filmmaking which many Europeans have avoided for fear of being too simple."[19] While conceiving *Show Me Love*, he associated filmmaking with a more open and public form of creative expression than poetry, which he sees as a private and introspective, even self-centered, activity. Yet, he expresses, "I have never really identified with the idea of my being a storyteller. I am more interested in details and in fragments."[20] Moodysson's self-presentation of his trajectory as a filmmaker is marked with ambivalence both toward the value of film as an expressive medium and toward his own status as acclaimed director. Indeed, a later film, like the low-budget and experimental *Container*, could be described as an anti-film: it is a poetic monologue in moving images.

Moodysson has often expressed ambivalence toward his role of director. He claims after each film, as did Ingmar Bergman, that it is to be his last one. In the PR material distributed to Swedish media before Moodysson began shooting *Together*, the follow-up film to *Show Me Love*, the director included a personal letter written in what appears to be a candid voice: "The level of confidence I have in myself goes up and down. A few days ago I thought the screenplay [for *Together*] was worthless, and that the film should be stopped, but then I changed a few things in the script, and today I think it is brilliant."[21] He has also repeatedly voiced insecurity about the cin-

Lukas Moodysson shooting *Show Me Love* in Trollhättan, Sweden. Still photography. Image reproduced by permission of Memfis Film.

ematic medium; as both he and his long-time producer Lars Jönsson affirm, the director was initially not entirely comfortable with the technical apparatus of filmmaking. Moodysson even describes himself as feeling like "an amateur" on the set of *Show Me Love*.[22] This stance, oscillating between self-affirmation and self-doubt, also plays into Moodysson's idea of authenticity; he is no run-of-the-mill director operating on autopilot. His self-presentation suggests that for him filmmaking is a serious personal undertaking that deeply reflects his sense of authentic selfhood as one that is inherently ambivalent.

Moodysson and Memfis

Moodysson has been able to channel his sense of uncertainty into a creative strategy. Part of his success is due to the fact that he has been able to work with a core group of people and institutions since graduating from film school. This group has been central for his development as a filmmaker and has provided a foundation for his experimentation. In particular, Moodysson has had the backing of legendary producer Lars Jönsson, the founder and CEO of the production company Memfis Film, for all his films. This has given him stable production parameters. While scouting around for new talent and new projects, Jönsson saw Moodysson's exam film at Dramatiska Institutet, *En uppgörelse i den undre världen* (*Settlement in the Underworld*), which featured well-known Swedish actor Stefan Sauk.[23] Jönsson knew of Moodysson from his time as a poet and as a member of *Malmöligan*. The two also share an outsider position with respect to the Stockholm film establishment—both have their roots in the southern province of Skåne and lived and worked in Göteborg at the beginning of their careers. Having seen Moodysson's short exam film, Jönsson suggested they discuss possibilities for future collaborations, and he eventually offered Moodysson the chance to make a short pilot film on the Memfis label. The two connected on the level of creating dialogue—one of Moodysson's strengths—and the pilot film became a joint project in developing Moodysson's storytelling skills. After multiple manuscript drafts, Moodysson shot *Talk* in Trollhättan (the home of regional film center Film i Väst).[24]

A continuing distinctive feature in the relationship between Moodysson and Jönsson has been storytelling and script development, with films like *Show Me Love* going through ten revisions and the much later *Mammoth* over twenty. *Together*, one of Moodysson's most successful films abroad, started with a fifty-page narrative with scattered thoughts that then went through multiple revisions to become a complete script. Moodysson confirms that this collaborative relationship with Jönsson has been critical to his development as a filmmaker: "Having just graduated from film school, I sent manuscripts to Lars [Jönsson] all the time, and he kept refusing to accept them. But he encouraged me to continue. And I felt strengthened by the fact that he wanted to read what I wrote. This attitude is unusual for a producer, and for most people I think, who want rapid and focused progression."[25] Jönsson speaks in complementary terms of his relationship to Moodysson: "At the time, I was looking for individual voices and independent storytellers. Developing a script and making a pilot film together gave us a chance to test each other out, to see if a long-term collaboration could be in the making."[26] Memfis, in contrast to many other contemporary Swedish production companies, has never pursued the model of adapting best-seller novels into films.[27] Some of its most successful collaborations and productions have instead been based on this model of developing concepts from scratch, providing mentorship, and cultivating long-term collaborative relationships. This is especially clear in the relationship between Memfis and Moodysson's early screenplays.

Script originality, including story arc and characterization, is central to Memfis productions, Jönsson affirms: "I want Memfis to be different, to be a small company with one or two quality productions a year." He continues, "I want to be closely involved in the aspects of filmmaking that shape the story: script development and final editing. Memfis works with filmmakers who are auteurs, who have a need to express themselves, who write for an audience, and whose stories I can help bring about. I have never been especially interested in the technical aspects of filmmaking and find film shoots utterly boring. I see my role as producer to identify and establish the right conditions for each director."[28] Jönsson's role for Moodysson cannot be overstated and includes sheltering Moodysson from direct engagement with funders, coproducers, and distributors. Jönsson emphasizes: "I have wanted to protect him from financial worry; I have wanted him to be 100 percent film artist in our collaboration. But we do work together very closely, and sometimes he argues for an economically motivated decision while I get totally consumed by a detail in the editing process."[29] This kind of stable relationship has established an updated form of the auteur paradigm for Moodysson, by which he as director and scriptwriter has a strong degree of autonomy and independence. There is no other contemporary Swedish film director who has had this kind of support from a production company in which he or she has no stake in ownership.

Memfis Film has played a significant role in the Swedish film industry since its inception in 1989. Several of its films make up the core of what is usually labeled as a golden era of Swedish film at the turn of the millennium.[30] Part of this success stems from the stable funding models Memfis has been able to establish. This includes investing its own funds as well as seeking support from the Swedish and Danish Film Institutes and coproducing with Danish Zentropa, the regional film center Film i Väst, and public service channel Svensk Television (SvT). Jönsson and Memfis both benefited from and contributed to developing a dynamic film production context during the mid-1990s and the first decade of the twenty-first century. This includes the transformation of funding models ushered in by the European coproduction agreement in 1992, the establishment of the Nordic Film and TV Fund (NFTF), the availability of regional coproduction funding from Film i Väst, at the time supported by the European Union, and capitalizing on the need for quality programming by the public television's drama department based in Göteborg (SvT). Lars Jönsson and Zentropa's Peter Aalbaek Jensen, friends and longtime collaborators, also jointly funded Trust Film Sales in the mid-1990s, which was to become the most important international distributor of Swedish and Danish film at the turn of the millennium. *Show Me Love* was one of the first films distributed internationally by Trust Film Sales. Jönsson's successful strategies for securing domestic and international funding and distribution have arguably allowed for the level of experimentation seen in Moodysson's films and the divergence between them—moving, for example, from the warm and upbeat *Together* to the bleak and forbidding *Lilya 4-ever*, or from the monologue of the video art–inspired *Container* to the international big-budget epic *Mammoth*. Moodysson is clearly an original filmmaker and a sophisticated storyteller, but part of his success is also based on the concrete support given to him by Memfis and its production infrastructure.

Cinema as a Collective Endeavor: Crew and Cast

Moodysson has been able to work with a largely stable group of film professionals, who have continued to make films with him over the years. Memfis producer Lars Jönsson is the most obvious example, but other key members in the film team have remained mostly consistent, though sometimes in changing, multiple roles. This team includes Malte Forsell (line producer and production manager), Michal Leszczylowski (editing), Ulf Brantås (photography), Malin Fornander (director's assistant and continuity), Josefin Åsberg (art direction/production design), Jesper Kurlandsky (casting, production assistance, and creative sparring), Kalle Strandlind (location manager), Anna Malini Ahlberg (production management and assistant producer), and Alexandra Dahlström (principal actor in *Show Me*

Love and involved in later films in casting and as production assistant). Film photographer Ulf Brantås shot the short film *Talk* and was instrumental in creating the distinctive look of Moodysson's first three feature films *Show Me Love*, *Together*, and *Lilya 4-ever*. The cinematography of these films includes distinctive crash zooms, close framing and blocking of characters within a frame, the use of practical light sources (rather than three-point spotlights), an emphasis on interior confinement, and a general avoidance, especially in *Show Me Love* and *Together*, of establishing shots for locations or landscapes that divert attention from characters. Brantås earned a *Guldbagge* for his cinematography on *Lilya 4-ever*, and the collaboration between Brantås and Moodysson made the director's first three feature films aesthetically distinctive.

Moodysson has repeatedly stressed in interviews how he perceives filmmaking as a collective enterprise, which also includes making compromises. The significance of editor Michal Leszczylowski, who was Moodysson's professor of editing at Dramatiska Institutet, has been especially significant in this regard. Leszczylowski, together with assistants, has edited all of Moodysson's films except *Container*. A principal contribution of Leszczylowski, often aided by Jönsson and in collaboration with Moodysson, has been his strategy of emphasizing narrative and character coherence in order to counterbalance Moodysson's propensity for fragmentation.[31] Moodysson has indicated an increasing understanding of filmmaking as a collaborative project, moving toward formulations that take into account that the perception of authenticity and realism is not the result of one singular vision but of a collective enterprise. Though strong-willed and dedicated to his artistic vision (as multiple collaborators attest), Moodysson also expresses a more pragmatic side: "I believe quite a bit in compromises. Meeting half way is usually the best strategy."[32]

Dahlström and Kurlandsky, both of whom began working with Moodysson and Memfis in their teens, also express their appreciation for inclusion in the filmmaking process as collaborators. For them, Moodysson has become a mentor and a friend in the process, and they both credit him with having had a formative influence on their subsequent careers as actor and director (Dahlström) and producer (Kurlandsky). As a film practitioner Moodysson has over time become deeply engaged in all artistic aspects of the production—from script development, casting, and, in some cases, camera operation to final editing. Though keeping the team around Moodysson small and stable was indeed part of Memfis' strategy for the early part of his career, Moodysson's involvement in all artistic aspects of the filmmaking process also testifies to his status as a European auteur.

When Moodysson reflects on *Show Me Love*, he emphasizes the significance of its dialogue, of wanting the spoken word to sound authentic.[33] Dialogue rather than storyboarding has been a primary vehicle for Moodysson as a director. Though his screenplays are specific and detailed, they are "based on dialogue. I try to be very precise and simple when I write," and he indicates "very few camera movements."[34] Moodysson affirms that actors' voices are critical to him during the filming process and that he focuses on their formulation of lines rather than visual appearance.[35] "I know what is authentic and feels true," Moodysson says. "I could work as a lie detector at a prosecution." Part of Moodysson's self-presentation as a director thus appears to involve maintaining a sense of connection with poetic expression, of seeking to find the right word at the right moment, and of emphasizing the sound and cadence of speech as markers of authenticity. Moodysson's screenplays have also been adapted for the stage and produced around Europe; their authentic-sounding dialogue is arguably one of the reasons for theater interest in his work.[36]

Speaking about himself as a director, Moodysson has expressed how central casting has been to his mission. "I am good at working with actors and with selecting actors for parts. I feel like this is one of my strongest assets as director."[37] His style has also been marked by a general reluctance at structuring rehearsals or guiding movements:

> I want to give actors freedom, and I look for moments when they surprise me and do the unexpected. I have always felt it to be terribly delimiting to structure movement and gesture according to tape marks on the floor; sometimes my actors are out of focus or block one another, but I prefer that style. It feels more authentic. Similarly, I want to be physically present as a director. I do not believe in a division between those who do the physical labor—photographers and actors—and the director. I cannot sit in a corner and call out directions. I need to be right there.[38]

The collaborative aspect during filming has been critical to a number of his films. As a director, Moodysson follows his script but allows for some improvisation. This has been particularly important in screenplays translated from Swedish into Russian (*Lilya 4-ever*) and English *(Mammoth)*, where Moodysson affirms that actors have a strong say in the final formulation of their lines—he wants the lines to sound authentic to the actor who expresses them.[39]

The Figure of the Young Woman

A distinguishing feature of Moodysson's career has been its diversity in terms of film topics, genres, and aesthetic strategies. His most significant contribution in the context of Swedish film history, however, is his interest in a sustained and serious investigation of gender and sexuality. Moodysson's refusal to recast actors contributes to their distinctiveness, though the figuration of young women remains central in his films. As actor and director Alexandra Dahlström notes, several of Moodysson's leading actors resemble one another (Dahlström played Elin in *Show Me Love*): "Sanna Bråding [*Hole in My Heart*] and I look alike—curvy blondes—and Oksana Akinshina [*Lilya 4-ever*] and Run Srinikornchot [Cookie in *Mammoth*] are like peas in the pod. We look alike: Photogenic with high cheekbones and a distinctive profile. Looks may be similar, but Lukas has a way of portraying really strong young women. It is almost as if we become the same woman."[40] Dahlström's remarks point to a consistently significant feature of Moodysson's films, namely his interest in women's lives, especially adolescents and young women. This interest makes Moodysson unusual, particularly in relation to other contemporary male Swedish filmmakers who tend to focus on male protagonists (just as the number of male directors making feature films remains disproportionately high).

Dahlström's comments obliquely reflect the idea of a young woman archetype in Moodysson's films. The films invite us to explore the lives and perspectives of young women, which, in turn, help us understand the aesthetic, social, and gendered tensions he portrays. Women adolescents are privileged vehicles for accessing or enacting an ideology of authenticity in cinematic form, yet the filmmaker's personal identity as an adult male creates a layered and contradictory attitude. Similarly, the sexual experiences of young women and adolescents in his films offer what appears as an effort to capture an occasionally naïve essentialism of the young woman figure—innocent, yet taunting; virginal, yet seductive. At the same time, Moodysson's films engage explicitly with social, political, and economic ramifications that influence gender dynamics and, in particular, female sexuality, whether in the form of small-town suppression of lesbian attraction (*Show Me Love*), human trafficking (*Lilya 4-ever*), the pornography industry (*A Hole in My Heart*), transsexualism (*Container*), or prostitution and women's migrant labor (*Mammoth*). Moodysson's films posit that gender and sexuality must be analyzed in order for us to understand our world and aesthetic representations of it.

Local and Global: Production Design and Production Models

Cast and crew who have worked with Moodysson affirm his dedication to the authenticity and realism of production design and props. Moodysson's attention to place and locality is indeed one of his most distinctive features. "I am extremely interested in how people live and where people live. One of my biggest inspirations is just looking at different houses and looking at different areas and imagining how people live there: what kind of furniture they have and what it is like to grow up there and what it is like to be forty-five and alone in a place like that."[41] Attention to production design has involved minute preproduction on-location research for all his features. The careful research also helps establish a strong correlation between Moodysson's films as reflections of and commentaries on contemporary Sweden. *Show Me Love*, for example, was filmed nearly exclusively on-location. When shooting night scenes in Agnes' home, the crew had to wake up the inhabitant of the house they were borrowing because his snoring disturbed the sound recording; Elin's room in the same film was decorated by the local actors who play her friends in order to make it authentically reflect the location in which it was shot. *Together*'s collective house was fully inhabitable, and the actors could use the bathroom on set if they so wanted. In *Lilya 4-ever*, sequences shot in studio in Sweden were stocked with props transported from Estonia. In *A Hole in My Heart*, the production was framed as an on-location experiment. Some members of the cast and crew rarely left the set and the adjacent apartment, where they were living communally for the duration of the film shoot. For *Mammoth*, significant time was spent researching which kind of high-end chef's knives were to be featured in the affluent New York City kitchen. Moodysson's interest in the materiality of location has other ramifications as well. Though many of his films feature international settings, he shot all of his films at least partly in Trollhättan, the location of the regional film production center Film i Väst.

Strongly invested in the idea of location and place-specificity, Moodysson is also one of the most international of Swedish feature film directors of his generation, which has otherwise generally focused on making films set in Sweden. Following the Swedish focus of *Show Me Love* and *Together*, Moodysson began exploring explicitly international topics in his films, including moving filming locations to Estonia, Romania, Russia, the United States, the Philippines, and Thailand, and shooting his films in languages other than Swedish—Russian in *Lilya-4 ever* and English, Thai, and Tagalog in *Mammoth*. Moodysson is one of few contemporary Swedish directors to take on topics of world significance, including unequal distribution of wealth and, in particular, the abuse of non-Western women in schemes of trafficking, prostitution, and domestic labor. *Lilya 4-ever*, for example, illustrates the downside of a neoliberal worldview that promotes the free movement of goods and people across boundaries (Lilya is abandoned by her mother, who leaves to seek a new life in the United States). The ensuing story of Lilya's life mirrors the decline of the Soviet state into dissolution, despair, and post-Glasnost ruin. *Mammoth* includes the figure of Thai prostitute Cookie (Run

Srinikornchot) and Filipino maid Gloria (Marife Necesito), who put an individualistic and consumer-driven Western culture into sharp relief, and whose acting performances outshine those of their better-known Western colleagues (Gael García Bernal and Michelle Williams). Moodysson's Danish cinematographer in *Mammoth*, Marcel Zyskind, employs a wide lens modeled on cinemascope. Though the film is full of close-ups, Zyskind's camera tends to situate the characters against a spatial and social context. *Mammoth*, Moodysson remarks, was an exception to his cinematic oeuvre, however: "The production apparatus was too large, it became too expensive, and too complicated. Filming in four countries, with a large cast and crew, and with intertwined story lines was too much. I am interested in Sweden again."[42] Implicit in Moodysson's remarks about *Mammoth* in related interviews is a sentiment that the film's authenticity was being diluted by the circumstances created by the large-scale production.

Moodysson and Scandinavian Film

Moodysson's films contributed to the rejuvenation of Swedish cinema at the end of the 1990s, at the time when new Danish cinema—including Dogme 95 films by Lars von Trier, Thomas Vinterberg, and Lone Scherfig—was making waves around the world.[43] In the international press, *Show Me Love* was often seen as related to this group of films, though Moodysson rejects any influence. In fact, Jönsson had initially wanted Moodysson to consider making a Dogme 95 film, but Moodysson is reputed to have said that he refused following in the footsteps of anyone else and that he considered the Dogme 95 manifesto "extremely silly."[44] Connections between Moodysson and von Trier are prevalent, however, not least by virtue of the close collaborations between the production companies that have backed their respective films. Though the directors live close to each other (Malmö and Copenhagen) and have shot extensively in Trollhättan (where von Trier filmed *Dancer in the Dark*, 2000; *Dogville*, 2003; and *Manderlay*, 2005), they do not know one another. There are intriguing parallels, nevertheless. One involves a material connection. Moodysson began shooting *Together* right after von Trier had finished *Dancer in the Dark*. He reflects on this as a coincidence: "[On] one of our cameras it said 'Lars's machine.' I erased that and etched 'Lukas's machine' instead. It was quite comic."[45] Other significant connections involve their shared interest in experimentation and the fact that they have addressed similar topics with divergent aesthetic measures throughout their careers. Moodysson's *Together*, like von Trier's *The Idiots* (*Idioterne*, 1998, unattributed), is a story about a collective and an allegorical retelling of fraught national identity conveyed through the perspective of outsiders. Von Trier's detached take on a young woman's slide into delusions and prostitution in *Breaking the Waves* (1996) differs remarkably from Moodysson's soul-searing portrayal of a similar theme in *Lilya 4-ever* (2002).

Moodysson's appraisal of von Trier centers on his understanding of the Danish director as less interested in affective or social authenticity: "I think about *The Idiots* approximately what I think of the rest of von Trier's production. He is a genius and he is innovative, but he doesn't move me."[46] Moodysson and von Trier do share an explicit interest in renouncing Scandinavian cinema's reliance on costume dramas, heritage films, and literary adaptations during the 1980s and 1990s, as exemplified by the successful international export of Gabriel Axel's *Babette's Feast* (*Babettes gæstebud*, 1988).[47] In *Show Me Love*, Moodysson almost completely renounces establishing landscape shots, and *A Hole in My Heart* is set nearly exclusively in an apartment in an anonymous multistory 1970s-era housing complex. Von Trier's historical drama *Dogville* is set in a fictional Colorado town in the 1930s and shot on an enormous Trollhättan sound stage where white marks on the floor outline buildings and landscape features. Neither Moodysson nor von Trier is especially interested in experimenting with either natural landscape shots or light, thus breaking a long tradition in Scandinavian cinema. The aesthetic and cultural ramifications of natural Nordic light have been significant since the silent cinema of Victor Sjöström, Mauritz Stiller, and Carl Theodor Dreyer. The idea of natural Nordic light achieved a cultural and aesthetic high point in the celebrated luminescence of Sven Nykvist's cinematography for Ingmar Bergman, demonstrated in classics such as *Through a Glass Darkly* (*Såsom i en spegel*, 1961) and *Persona* (1966). Several of Moodysson's and von Trier's experimental films involve an oblique commentary on Scandinavia's privileged position in the world, as seemingly sheltered from social inequality, war and violence, and environmental destruction, yet neither directly addresses Scandinavia's status as a multiethnic region of the world. I will return to address this topic later.

Though Moodysson has repeatedly rejected any explicit influence from Ingmar Bergman, there are, in fact, significant connections that I explore in more detail in chapters 2 and 3 of this book.[48] Moodysson is the closest thing to an auteur figure of international stature in recent Swedish cinema. Moodysson interrogates and re-imagines classic Bergman tropes and themes, from the attraction between two women in *Show Me Love*—ambivalently portrayed in central Bergman films like *Three Strange Loves* (*Törst*, 1949), *The Silence* (*Tystnaden*, 1963), *Persona* (1966), and *Cries and Whispers* (*Viskningar och rop*, 1973)—to his explicit investigation of the mid-1970s Swedish welfare state in *Together*. The welfare state is a topic Bergman never explicitly addresses, but it is obliquely present in a number of his films, including *Scenes from a Marriage* (*Scener ur ett äktenskap*, 1973). Moodysson also offers an intriguing reinterpretation of the chamber play structure in *A Hole in My Heart*, whose four principal characters, tormented by anxiety and confined to interaction in one domestic setting during a short time span, appear to be indirect references to *Through a Glass Darkly* and *Cries and Whispers*. Moodysson's interest in verisimilitude and social realism also seems to draw from a long list of acclaimed Swedish directors, such as Bo Widerberg, Stefan Jarl, and Jan Troell, who provided a counterpart to Ingmar Bergman's introspective, dense, and existential films of the 1960s and 1970s. Likewise, Moodysson's interest in different conceptualizations of sexualities and gender relations tie his films to a large number of Swedish filmmakers from an earlier generation and known outside of Sweden, including Mai Zetterling, Vilgot Sjöman, and Ingmar Bergman. His interest in childhood and adolescence also reflects a cinematic tradition particularly strong in the Swedish tradition, including such well-known exports as Lasse Hallström's *My Life as a Dog* (*Mitt liv som hund*, 1987) and Ingmar Bergman's final feature film for wide cinema distribution, *Fanny and Alexander* (*Fanny och Alexander*, 1982).

Situating *Show Me Love* and Moodysson's oeuvre in a trajectory of well-known Swedish and Scandinavian filmmakers reveals his work as part of a history of films in national and transnational contexts and in unique conditions of production. These circumstances are significant for understanding how Moodysson's films engage gender and sexuality as well as location and spatiality beyond national borders.

2

The Ambivalence of *Show Me Love*

The Gaze

About five minutes into *Show Me Love* (*Fucking Åmål*, 1998), we encounter a striking scene. The setting is mundane and realistically represented—a noisy recess in a high school hallway lined with rows of identical lockers. Agnes, the brainy, intellectual outsider protagonist, is reluctantly distributing a birthday party invitation to her wheelchair-bound friend, Viktoria. The piece of paper is snapped up by one of the bullies in a clique of popular girls; she shrieks with scorn and contempt at the very thought of Agnes hosting a party that anyone would want to attend. This scene could be culled from a number of high school films, and we can recognize its dramatic intensity and characters as belonging to a set of conventions—the clique bully, the outsider nerd, the odd one out, and the social pressure created by the context. But the intensity of this scene is created only partly by plot and dialogue. It is augmented by a parallel shot construction that tells us that there is something else going on as well. Agnes does not look at her tormentors. Instead her gaze is fixed on another young woman. This is Elin, who rushes into the frame to hug Jessica, her older sister. Agnes' gaze lingers on Elin, the object of her desire, while Elin speaks with her sister. In this remarkable sequence, Moodysson reverses the heteronormative gaze, part of the bedrock of Hollywood conventions, which puts a desired female on display for "the gaze and enjoyment of men."[1] In Laura Mulvey's analysis, the heteronormative gaze serves up women to the camera/man as objects to be consumed through looking. A queering of that relationship (man/viewer/camera vs. woman/object) involves a different gender configuration and a different position of the camera, one that does not show the object of desire but rather the person who desires. This queering of the gaze involves putting the object of the gaze beyond the view of the audience so that we see its effect upon the gazer. *Show Me Love* reverses a heteronormative gaze and visually *queers* the movie. Moodysson uses this strategy repeatedly to represent the love story between the two young women.

Show Me Love is unique in a Swedish context and stands up to international comparison. Lukas Moodysson is one of a few male directors to make a film about young women as a debut feature production. This is a serious film about young women falling in love, and one in which they are not sexualized for the benefit of the male gaze. At the same time, Moodysson has continually expressed his ambivalence toward being associated with the lesbian content of the plot.[2] In an interview, he emphasizes, "That it became a love story in the way it did was never something I really intended. And I cannot remember how it turned out this way. Writing the script was about getting the dialogue right and situations authentically portrayed, and the story line seemed to have developed as part of a creative process that wasn't part of any original grand plan."[3] His initial interest was in writing a script about two sisters and their lives in a small town. In interviews at the time of the film's national and international

Challenging the heteronormative gaze? Agnes (Rebecka Liljeberg) looking at Elin (Alexandra Dahlström). Still photography by Åke Ottoson. Image reproduced by permission of Memfis Film.

releases, Moodysson and the two main actors, Alexandra Dahlström (Elin) and Rebecka Liljeberg (Agnes), emphatically downplayed the plot motivation and theme of same-sex desire. On the other hand, Moodysson has emphasized that filmmaking can make a difference both on the individual and sociopolitical level. One of his ambitions is to reach people and instill change, including overcoming prejudice

Agnes (Rebecka Liljeberg) in one of several close-ups looking at Elin (Alexandra Dahlström). Frame grab. Image reproduced by permission of Memfis Film.

and discrimination against homosexuality. Thus, an intriguing contradiction remains integral to the film: Moodysson is apparently not "intending" to make Sweden's first lesbian coming-out film, yet he is defacto making one.

Coming of Age and Coming Out: Sweden's First Lesbian Romance

Show Me Love is Sweden's first and until recently only lesbian coming-out story.[4] It has become a cult film of modern European and international gay cinema. *Show Me Love* is both a coming-of-age and a coming-out story, simultaneously a Hollywood-inspired high school film and a serious feature that foregrounds lesbian romance. It oscillates between convention and innovation, between the mundane and the unusual, and between conformity and radicalism. The film is a product of its time and place—small-town Sweden in the late 1990s—yet its reach extends far beyond national borders. Its complexity derives from the multiple levels of character portrayal, genre references, aesthetics, allusions to Swedish film history, the conditions of production, and divergent receptions by audiences and reviewers in Sweden and all over the world—most notably its Teddy Award for Best Gay and Lesbian Film at the Berlin Film Festival in 1999 and subsequent screenings at dozens of international gay and lesbian film festivals. This chapter seeks to tease out exactly what it is in this multilayered mix that has made the film a classic.

Agnes' expression of her love for Elin is the film's literal starting point. Before the title and opening credits, we hear the sound of a keyboard typing. The first shot in the film is of hands typing, from which the camera pans to Agnes' face. The camera cuts to a computer screen, where we read the following: "My Secret List. 1. I don't want to have a party. 2. Elin will see me [intermittent cut to camera facing Agnes as she types] 3. Elin will fall in love with me. I LOVE ELIN!!!!!!" The power of the gaze is immediately introduced in the film, by a meta-cinematic gesture, expressed literally in the Swedish as "att Elin skall titta på mig" (that Elin will look at me). Moodysson contrasts this gesture with explicit attention to the function of journal writing. On the one hand, this use of text in the cinematic medium is conventional. There is a long-established tradition of using narrative voice-over to give plot or character background and to establish connections to a character. This technique relates back to an earlier convention of cinematic representation that uses a written text, such as a letter, as an introduction to the cinematic universe. On the other hand, since we as viewers are aware of *who* is writing this journal entry, we are jolted out of conventional assumptions—this is a young woman writing a declaration of love for another young woman. The viewer gains intimacy with Agnes right away by reading her secret. The diary, intercut with shots of her face, further establishes an immediate point of connection between the viewer and Agnes.

The next scene, after the credits, establishes a distance from its characters—it jolts the viewer into a heated breakfast argument between Elin and her sister Jessica (Erica Carlson), in which the camera moves quickly and pans back and forth, up and down, and is slightly out of focus. This jarring scene climaxes with a screaming Elin dumping a glass of chocolate milk over her sister's head and throwing an empty box of cocoa at her. Their mother, exasperated and tired from having worked the night shift, demands to know exactly what is going on. In the juxtaposition of these scenes, Agnes is introduced as silent and introspective but expressive (she attaches words to her feelings) and Elin as loud and physical but inarticulate (screaming her frustration and throwing objects). Gendered and class clues are deftly established—Agnes has her own computer and writes her diary in the solitary quietude of her room; she is fully dressed without makeup, while Elin is part of a collective of women in a kitchen, all wearing bathrobes or nightclothes and not yet made up for the day. This juxtaposition quickly and effectively sets up a paradigm of oppositions out of which the film will attempt to release itself. Neither character nor the implied subject (spectator) position remains stable. Similarly, the film exercises multiple strategies to destabilize genre conventions between youth "fluff" and "serious" drama for adults, and sexual conventions between straight and gay.

The film unfolds during a tumultuous week in the lives of the two protagonists, 16-year-old Agnes and 14-year-old Elin. The two interact with a number of compelling secondary characters, particularly Elin's older sister Jessica, her boyfriend Markus, and his friend Johan, as well as Agnes' classmate Viktoria. The film is set in Åmål, a generic small town in the rural province of Dalsland, located west of Sweden's capital Stockholm, about four hours by car. The film was shot in the small town of Trollhättan, a little over an hour's drive south of the setting of Åmål.[5] Locations we encounter in *Show Me Love* are entirely mundane—the local high school, Agnes' family's house in a nice part of town, Elin's mother's small apartment in a 1970s building, a playground, a classmate's home (the scene of a drunken party), a hockey rink, and the bridge over the highway leading to Stockholm, which Elin crosses multiple times.

Told chronologically, the story's significant plot events unfold in a tightly constructed narrative arc, as indicated by this brief plot synopsis: We get to know the characters initially in their homes—Elin arguing with her sister over breakfast, while Agnes gets a traditional Swedish strawberry cake and gifts while still in bed on the morning of her sixteenth birthday. The scenes following are set in the high school and introduce all major characters, as well as visually exposing Agnes' desire for Elin in the invitation scene mentioned above. Frustrated by the town's lack of entertainment on a Friday night, Elin drags her sister Jessica to Agnes' party. Jessica initially protests because of Agnes' reputation as a lesbian. Elin defiantly offers that she "think[s] it is cool [to be lesbian]." At Agnes' house, the two sisters lock themselves in Agnes' room—leaving Agnes out. Elin initiates a bet with Jessica that she will kiss Agnes, and Jessica agrees to pay her pocket change if she does. Elin abruptly presses a kiss upon Agnes and then the two sisters burst out of the house and leave for a teen party at another friend's home. Elin thus expresses initial interest in Agnes, but it is characteristically ambiguous. At the friend's party, Elin is ogled by Johan and drinks herself sick on cheap wine. She throws up in a small bathroom, assisted by Johan, who proclaims that even after vomiting, he finds her "so damn beautiful." Elin leaves the party, heading back to Agnes' house. Humiliated by Elin's kiss and quick, giggling departure, Agnes has in the meantime cut her wrist. Elin's arrival inadvertently disrupts the suicide attempt. She returns to apologize. They go on a late-night walk, where they begin to get to know one another. Elin urges Agnes to stop a car so that they can both escape to Stockholm. In the back seat they kiss and get thrown out by the driver. Though Elin promises to call Agnes the next day, she does not. Instead she gets together with Johan. She has her first heterosexual intercourse with him, but then breaks up with him soon after.[6] Agnes, hurt and angry, eventually confronts Elin at the high school cafeteria, and they end up discussing their situation in a locked bathroom, where Elin confesses her love and desire for Agnes. At the end of the film, the two girls emerge triumphantly, and symbolically, from a small closeted space in which they have been hiding, and walk through the raucous and aggressive teen crowd. The final scene in the film shows the two girls chatting on Elin's bed at home, drinking chocolate milk.

Not Really Gay? Reception and Legacy

The success of this film was astonishing given its unique plot, unknown actors with regional dialects, the small-town setting, the limited budget (9.4 million SEK—about 1 million USD), and the fact that this was a debut feature by a young director. Over 870,000 tickets were sold in Sweden, which is an unusually high number for a population of less than 9 million.[7] Lars Jönsson, the film's producer and CEO of the then up-and-coming production company Memfis

Film, worked closely with Peter Possne at the Swedish distributor, Sonet Film, in pitching *Show Me Love* to a number of media outlets, where it received extensive exposure. Pre-release press coverage was extensive, including spreads in major Stockholm-based newspapers such as *Svenska Dagbladet*, *Dagens Nyheter*, and *Expressen*. The film premiered on October 23, 1998. Swedish critics generally raved about *Show Me Love*, and reviews indicate that critics perceived it as a landmark in the country's film history.[8] The film immediately became a blockbuster hit. It won four *Guldbagge* awards in the national award ceremony the following year, for best film, director, and actors, and was also chosen to represent Sweden for the Academy Award foreign film nominations (it did not get selected as a finalist). Remarks by Charlotta Denward of the Swedish Film Institute (SFI) help clarify its position and legacy in the Swedish film landscape of the 1990s. The screenplay struck her as "fresh and unusual—it was a film about youth that did not feature male protagonists or a violent suburban context of drugs and weapons, but instead focused on the overlooked—the small town in the province—and, most of all, on strong young female characters in a story that emphasized realistic and authentic experiences."[9]

In preparation for international distribution Memfis decided to change Moodysson's title before it screened all over Europe in 1999–2000, as well as in North America, Australia, and New Zealand. In Sweden the film was released and continues to be known as *Fucking Åmål*, with the expletive referring to Elin's frustration that her small town has nothing going for it—to her, it is not only a backwater, it is "fucking damn cock Åmål," a literal translation of Moodysson's script: "fucking jävla kuk-Åmål" (the English subtitles read "fucking motherfuck Åmål"). The Åmål locale defines the Swedish title—indeed, it seems to signal that the film's central aspect is life in this particular small town—but this implication is erased in the international English title. "Fucking" is a generic discursive amplifier in contemporary informal Swedish, but the use of an Anglicism also locates the film as part of international youth culture facilitated by World English. The title *Show Me Love* is, on the one hand, vague and generic—a kind of whitewashing of the intensity of the Swedish title. On the other hand, the English title explicitly labels the film a love story, and suggests that love can have a performative element— it can be enacted, demonstrated, and repeated: "shown." The love suggested in the English title is not inherent or stable but, we could presume, a messy aggregate of emotions and actions, which is exactly what the two characters Agnes and Elin demonstrate to each other.[10]

The title *Show Me Love* comes from the title of the song played during the end credits; this song was offered to Moodysson for use in the film by Swedish pop singer Robyn. In 1997, "Show Me Love" had reached number seven on the Billboard list. Robyn, like the youth group Ace of Base, is part of a group of successful Swedish pop icons of the 1990s, whose songs were played widely in the US, and who had a gay following (ABBA's international camp hit status is another possible connection). Robyn is a popular culture icon in Sweden. She began recording music at age 12, producing several domestic top-ten hits by age 16. Robyn's image, moreover, makes a cameo appearance in *Show Me Love* on the bottle of "Robyn" perfume given to Agnes as a birthday present from Viktoria. Robyn is Elin's favorite singer; Agnes cannot stand her. As a pop icon, Robyn spans the age group and topics of the film; her international success also helps situate *Show Me Love* in a cultural context that extends beyond the borders of Sweden and, indeed, beyond the small town of Åmål. In contrast, maintaining the title "Fucking Amal" would have violated profanity standards in certain countries, and without the diacritical marks it could also suggest, as a critic in the *Village Voice* remarked, that the film is "Turkish gay porn."[11] This possible implication gives the film another queer connotation in an international context.

The title in Swedish, moreover, can be misleading. Agnes and Elin kiss on only two occasions, and any explicit sexual activity is absent. The film challenges the heteronormative paradigm. Spectators do not get a cathartic resolution or a sense of closure according to the Hollywood model for depicting romantic relationships. Moodysson allows the emerging relationship between the two young women to evolve without a grand finale kiss or sexual act.

Promotional posters and other visual material used to market *Show Me Love* domestically and internationally indicate further tension about how to position the film. The first poster version, used to market the film in Sweden for its premiere in 1998, is dark and grainy. It shows Agnes and Elin on a highway bridge at night: Elin scantily clad in a tight red camisole top and short skirt; Agnes in a bulky sweatshirt and army pants. The girls look hesitant and aloof, and the imagery is suggestive. What are the two seemingly incompatible young women doing alone late at night in this location? What draws them together, or seems to push them apart? Above the title, a close-up of Elin's face is bathed in warm light. For the UK and US releases, promotional material shows the two girls seated close to each other, intimate and laughing. In these pictures, Elin wears the same revealing red top, with Agnes dressed in what could be a man's checkered work shirt. A remarkably different Swedish poster shows Agnes and Elin with other major teen characters in the film—Jessica, Johan, and Markus—intercut against strips of green. Elin and Johan are positioned together in the center of the image. This poster transforms the focus on the two girls to one that suggests a teen movie with multiple characters. *Show Me Love*'s production company,

The first Swedish promotional poster of *Show Me Love* emphasizes the relationship between Agnes (Rebecka Liljeberg) and Elin (Alexandra Dahlström). It also accentuates the film's symbolic use of a bridge, which the girls cross several times in the film as their relationship evolves. Image reproduced by permission of Memfis Film.

The US promotional poster suggests that this is a film primarily about Elin (Alexandra Dahlström) but maintains a focus on her relationship with Agnes (Rebecka Liljeberg), portraying them as intimate. Image reproduced with permission. Poster art, Strand Releasing US rights.

THE AMBIVALENCE OF *SHOW ME LOVE*   39

The second Swedish promotional poster for *Show Me Love* presents the film as more of a traditional youth film about a collective of teenagers with Elin's (Alexandra Dahlström) relationship to Johan (Mattias Hult) in the center strip. Image reproduced by permission of Memfis Film.

Memfis Film, was closely involved in the marketing strategies of the film, designing the material, cutting trailers, and deciding on primary media outlets.[12] Memfis and Swedish distributor Sonet Film interwove both Swedish poster versions in their marketing of the film, indicating awareness that *Show Me Love* straddles several genres and audience expectations.

Memfis' marketing strategies for domestic and international audiences provides a backdrop to the film's critical reception in Sweden. Reviews in the Swedish media generally praised the authenticity of the script, acting, directing, and dialogue, and some commented on the immediacy of its cinematic form (quick cuts, zooms, an active camera) that draws the viewer in. Initial interpretations framed the central issues of the film as common teenage frustrations, including outsider status, budding sexuality, the stifling environment of a small town, the generation gap, and so forth. Few reviewers acknowledged, however, that this is a film specifically about same-sex desire, about two young women falling in love who declare their desires to the world, and not just any story about high school youth or small-town life. After six successful weeks at the box office, Karin Thunberg, a critic in the reputable and widely circulated daily *Svenska Dagbladet*, asks the first critical question about the film's skewed reception in an article titled "Vart tog deras lesbiska kärlek vägen?" (What happened to their lesbian love?).[13]

In fact, the majority of Swedish critical responses to *Show Me Love* implied, in most instances, that the film was universal because it was not *really* about lesbianism.[14] Tiina Rosenberg, Sweden's leading queer theory scholar, argues that the critical silence makes evident Swedish mainstream culture's oppressive heteronormative baseline with respect to lesbian content, especially given the unusually large number of films with gay male content that actually premiered in Sweden the same year.[15] A much-debated photography exhibit became a rallying point for the LGBT presence in Swedish culture around the same time. Elisabeth Ohlson's photography exhibit *Ecce Homo* showed Jesus in a number of biblical situations that brought a queer sensibility to the art scene. One photograph, for example, depicts a last meal with Jesus surrounded by cross-dressing apostles and a Pietà in which Jesus appears to be dying from AIDS.[16] In contrast to this hotly debated exhibit, the silencing of the lesbian love story in *Show Me Love* turns on its head the cultural stereotype of Swedes, projected domestically as well as internationally, as both politically liberal and sexually open-minded. In a global context, Sweden has been at the forefront in terms of gay rights. Since 1995, same-sex couples have been able to register as domestic partners with nearly equal rights as married heterosexual couples; same-sex couples have equal rights as prospective adoptive parents, lesbian couples can apply for assisted conception at state hospitals, and in 2009 marriage officially became gender-neutral in Sweden. *Show Me Love* evokes a contemporary social and cultural ambivalence with respect to gay rights and to the presence of queer cultural representation in Sweden. On the one hand, the film exemplifies the country's traditionally progressive policies on gender and sexuality issues. On the other hand, its reception shows a persistence in marginalizing attitudes toward same-sex desire when it comes to women.

The cultural impact of *Show Me Love* for young women in Sweden and elsewhere has been significant. Several journalists and writers who contributed to the best-seller collection of feminist essays *Fittstim* reported that *Show Me Love* had a transformative impact on their lives—it made life as a young lesbian imaginable.[17] Similarly, director Lukas Moodysson and actor Dahlström report that they have had letters sent to them from all over the world, telling about the fundamental significance this film has had on people's lives.[18] The release of the film also coincided with the popularization of queer theory in Sweden at the end of the 1990s, including an early adaptation of Judith Butler's theories in courses on gender and women's studies; in 2002, Butler was invited by a cohort of Swedish scholars to give lectures, during which she was greeted like a rock star.[19] So though there was an initial critical silencing of the same-sex theme in mainstream venues, contemporary representations of queer and lesbian culture provides a rich subtext. Moodysson's film was extremely timely: through a mainstream form accessible to a broad Swedish audience, it addresses gender and sexuality, topics that avant-garde artists, academic cultural critics, and other Hollywood films released in Sweden around the same time were also making visible.

Show Me Love is both queer and heteronormative. It is a coming-out story, in which conventional gender roles are, in fact, repeatedly affirmed and the status quo is maintained. The fact that critics initially chose not to emphasize the film's explicit charting of same-sex desire also testifies to the film's complexity. It is *queer* in the sense of queer theory's most basic definition of queerness or queering as investigating alternatives to the normative. But the film depends on double registers, which allow a spectator to situate the story within a heteronormative framework. Seen from this perspective, the film is not "really" about lesbian attraction but is instead representative of a conventional heterosexual Western romance plot with a narrative arc, in which two characters overcome hurdles in order to become a couple.[20] Still, *Show Me Love* is a classic within Swedish film, and more broadly within European and US film, due to the multiple interpretive levels with respect to gender and sexuality. They contribute to the film's narrative and aesthetic complexity as conveyed through the dialogue, locations, and cinematography.

Crossing Over and Aesthetic Reversals

Though a lot of the significant action in *Show Me Love* takes place in interiors—including in bathrooms, small bedrooms, and classrooms that emphasize a sense of claustrophobia and confinement—a critical site in the film is the bridge that crosses over the highway to Stockholm. Elin crosses this bridge four times in the film; once she and Agnes walk it together late at night after Elin has returned to Agnes' home to apologize for having smeared a kiss on her as part of a bet with her sister. The shot composition of Elin and Agnes crossing the bridge is striking. The young women emerge from the darkness and walk toward the streetlights. The image is grainy. Elin is talkative and spontaneous, without jacket, in her revealing red top and short black miniskirt; Agnes is quiet and reflective, walking next to her covered up in a bomber jacket and military pants. Crossing over a bridge—the symbolism of transformation is clear—the characters begin to get to know one another, though the dialogue is sparse. They talk about the future: Elin reveals her hopes of becoming a model, while Agnes claims that she wants to study psychology, but then affirms that she wants to be a writer. Elin expresses interest in this profession in this scene, which seems to be one of those moments where Elin's indecision and hesitation pops out (does she or can she know what she wants at age 14?); it seems related to her "promiscuity" (she has not slept with anyone but she's necked with 70,000, as Jessica says). Moodysson establishes the idea that she is trying out multiple possibilities rather than being constrained by one *straight* path.

Elin's hesitation and curiosity reflect the film's ambivalence toward issues of sexuality. Questioning the stability of sexual identities is an undercurrent in the film. Elin poses the film's significant questions directly to Agnes in the middle of the bridge: "Have you been with many girls?" Agnes answers, "No. You are the first I have kissed." Elin continues, "Are you lesbian?" (Agnes does not answer.) Then Elin affirms, "I think it is cool. I want to become one, too." Elin later in the same scene tries to put words to her understanding of Agnes' difference. "You are weird," she says. Agnes responds right away, "You're also weird." And Elin continues. "I want to be weird. Well, not weird, but . . . I don't want to be like everyone else. Though, sometimes I'm just the same." Agnes responds, "You're not." At the center of the bridge the camera cuts between the faces of the women in this symbolic sequence. This deceptively simple dialogue illustrates Moodysson's craft in foregrounding the screenplay's ambivalence toward questions of sexuality.

For the first time in the film, Elin seems to be intellectually and emotionally curious and receptive. She possesses an interest in an alternative or dynamic identity construction, but one that is contained and stabilized in the term "lesbian." Yet Agnes refuses to answer questions that would restrictively label her; instead, she responds only to inquiries about practices (kissing) and choices (paths of study or careers), and retorts that her life or preferences are not any stranger than the seemingly conventional path that Elin appears to have initially imagined for herself.

The highway to Stockholm triggers fantasies of an alternative to small-town limitations and heteronormative confinement. Elin, impulsive and exuberant after their initial talk, dares Agnes to hitchhike to Stockholm, with the implicit assumption that once there, the two can explore big city freedom. A car stops; the driver, a middle-aged man, appears particularly attracted to Elin in her red tank top. Seated in the backseat of a Saab 900, the two girls kiss for the second time with Foreigner's "I Want to Know What Love Is" blaring. Moodysson breaks the unspoken rule of mainstream heteronormative cinematic representation by showing two women kissing on screen and enjoying it. The fantasy of escape comes to an abrupt end as the driver of the car throws the two out, inquiring if they are pulling a joke on him: "Is this Candid Camera?" The end of this scene opens up a number of interpretations. The male character is figured as a traditional cinematic pervert—his gaunt-looking face and cold stare a version of a Peeping Tom who ogles a young Lolita in the back seat—and as the voice of heterosexual patriarchy and provinciality. If two women kiss, we may infer from his comment, it must be a joke, and the joke is on him. He is an on-screen representation of a traditional cinematic gaze as well as a physical obstruction to the young women's sexual exploration. This moment draws on the cinematic convention of a romantic "first kiss" between young protagonists (in this case it is the second, but the implications are clear), just as it momentarily puts the viewer in the perspective of the driver, the figure of the older, observing male who enacts the heteronormative gaze. The scene requests that we take a stance: Is our gaze one of queer acceptance, or is it one of heterosexual rejection? This scene is open to multiple interpretations, which is part of *Show Me Love*'s effectiveness.

Queer expressions of sexuality, as Jenny Björklund shows while elaborating on Judith Halberstam's *In a Queer Place and Time*, have been construed as the prerogative of the big city; *Show Me Love*, along the lines of Halberstam's rethinking of gay culture being relegated to the city, involves "a queering of the small town." [21] Their escape to Stockholm thwarted, Elin and Agnes express their desire here in Åmål.[22] On the other hand, after this scene, the two women walk their separate ways (they live on opposite sides of the highway to Stockholm), and Elin jumps into a relationship with Johan. This scene is indicative of Moodysson's strategy in *Show Me Love*, as it hovers between the conventional and the unconventional, between the daring and the traditional, between the queer and the heteronormative.

The dark and grainy night scene on the bridge and the reference to Candid Camera offer a relevant point for comparison between *Show Me Love* and well-known Dogme 95 films released the same year (1998)—*The Celebration (Festen)* by Thomas Vinterberg and *The Idiots (Idioterne)* by Lars von Trier—though both are officially uncredited, according to the Dogme 95 Manifesto, which precludes crediting the director.[23] Moodysson's film emphasizes authenticity, realism, and the everyday. As in Dogme 95, dialogue and acting are at the center of the story—there are no special effects, whether plot-driven or aesthetic—and the film skirts clear genre affiliations like the Dogme 95 manifesto instructs. It is also filmed nearly exclusively on location in authentic milieus with few noticeable cinematic tricks in terms of photography or editing. The camera moves and follows characters closely. *Show Me Love* is not a Dogme 95 film, however, and any influence from the Danish directors' manifesto has been repeatedly disavowed by both Moodysson (who emphasizes in interviews and in the commentary on the Swedish DVD of *Show Me Love* that he rarely uses a handheld camera, for example) and producer Lars Jönsson.[24] The visual aesthetics of the film likely strike a present-day audience as reminiscent of Dogme 95 films shot on digital video (e.g., Vinterberg's *The Celebration*), but this effect is largely achieved by the reverse film stock and the use of already existing light sources, called "practicals." Similarly, music is often diegetically triggered, such as in the scenes when Agnes listens to CDs in her room and when Elin and Agnes kiss in the backseat of a car, but, contrary to Dogme 95 guidelines, the soundtrack is obviously mixed in and enhanced later in the production process.

The visual aesthetics of the film illustrate both production and thematic contexts. A large number of scenes in *Show Me Love* are interior shots. One recurring setting is Agnes' bedroom, where the dark-blue walls seem to draw light away from the actors. In some instances, actors barely contrast with the background. Interiors seem grainy and underlit, as if they had been shot with digital video, with only natural or low-grade artificial lighting, by an amateur camera crew, or as part of an exercise in documentary filmmaking. In fact, *Show Me Love* was shot on 16-mm film, which allows for a smaller and more mobile camera than a traditional feature film format of 35 mm; it is also less expensive to procure and process than 35 mm. After being shot on 16 mm, the film was transferred to 35 mm for its theatrical release. The use of 16-mm

Agnes' (Rebecka Liljeberg) bedroom. One of many dark and underlit scenes set in mundane interiors. Still photography by Åke Ottoson. Image reproduced by permission of Memfis Film.

film fit nicely within the larger context of the film's production. The producer sought to keep the team as small as possible and the stress as low as possible for Moodysson's first feature film.[25] The cinematographer Ulf Brantås was closely involved in conceiving the film's visual aesthetics in Moodysson's first four films (the short *Talk* and the features *Show Me Love*, *Together*, and *Lilya 4-ever*). He explains how the film's color scheme and graininess stem from the fact that it is filmed on reverse film stock—an unusual process for feature-film production.[26] It involves filming on the positive and then developing that stock as a negative; after that a copy transferable to 35 mm is made. The film reacts differently to the colors blue and red in this process, which creates both an enhanced graininess and color saturation.[27] For a film like *Show Me Love*, which is precisely about showing relationships that had previously not been included in Swedish film, the process of reversing the actual film medium and using an unusual process seems singularly well suited to the film's central themes. The reverse film stock appears to "queer" the cinematography, and thus the departure from standard industry practice reflects the film's identity.

Moodysson had a very clear aesthetic model in mind for the film. He wanted a visual mix between Ellen von Unwerth's documentary style fashion photography in real settings with subdued contrast and enhanced graininess and the saturated color schemes of an American photographer of abandoned cars. (The photographer may have been Troy Paiva.) To the cinematographer Brantås, these two images seemed incompatible, but Moodysson affirmed that he wanted the film to look like a combination of the two. This juxtaposition of visual registers led Brantås to suggest the reverse film stock. Moodysson acknowledges that he may not have been fully aware of the implications of this choice. "I wanted the saturated colors and dynamic graininess of reversal process photography, but I wasn't fully aware of how this would work when moving images are projected."[28] Another implication was that the image quality is deemed inferior by many television channels, and for the subsequent re-release of the DVD in 2009, the production company Memfis had to tinker with the image quality to get it closer to acceptable standards.[29] Moodysson and Brantås affirm that viewer reactions to the visual style in letters, conversations, and blog posts have spanned from enthusiastic approval to hostile disapproval.[30]

The lighting in *Show Me Love* also contributes to its special visual aesthetics. It is conceived to look natural with hardly any three-point artificial light sources (key, fill, and back lighting) or reflectors, common in Hollywood films. Rather than a conventionally lit film, Moodysson wanted to use only practicals. The lighting contributes to the film's documentary look. But filming largely indoors—in small and sometimes dark bedrooms, tiny bathrooms, ordinary living rooms, and standard classrooms, etc.—put specific demands on lighting. At the same time the slower and reverse film stock demanded sufficient light in order to expose the images. This meant that cinematographer Brantås worked closely with scenographer Lina Strand to accommodate Moodysson's request for a natural style. For example, they changed all existing light sources to 250-watt bulbs and included more practicals placed around rooms in strategic ways. The camera was mostly positioned, Moodysson recalls, in a corner to allow the young actors as much freedom as possible to move. It was always stationary and on a tripod, never handheld. The suggestion of hand-held camera aesthetics are achieved through shot composition. In fact, a distinguishing feature of the film's aesthetic is its dependence on zooms and medium shots (an intermediary between a close-up and a full view), rather than long full views or tracking shots (when the camera is being moved on wheels to follow the action).

The shot composition in *Show Me Love* includes strategies that shape the aesthetics of the film and sustain both its apparent connections to Dogme 95 and its "home movie" illusion of authenticity. Moodysson recalls that he wanted flexibility of movement on set, and shied away from using tape markers on the floor or other similar measures in directing the actors and cinematographer. "With such young actors, and a small crew, I wanted freedom to experiment and feel the process out," Moodysson recalls, "and it was my first feature film. I am not sure I always knew what I was doing."[31] Director of photography Brantås recalls that he and Moodysson had relatively little discussion about the visual composition but reports that upon reading the manuscript he immediately decided that the camera had to be close to the two protagonists. "I did not want to lose the characters out of sight for a second," he explains. "I felt I wanted the camera to be in their zone, so that the viewer experiences them in their personal sphere. I try to think of myself as a fellow actor when I film, and I sought to be a partner to the actors."[32] Moodysson concurs, stating his view that Brantås has a "phenomenal presence" on the set and seems "to know instinctively how to follow actors closely."[33]

The use of crash zooms, in which the rapid refocusing of the lens causes the image to momentarily blur, is a distinguishing feature of *Show Me Love*. It is also used liberally in *Together* and to a certain extent in *Lilya 4-ever*. A feature of 1970s filmmaking, the use of crash zooms was unusual in Swedish and European film aesthetics at the end of the 1990s. As Moodysson emphasizes,

> I am fascinated by zooms, both theoretically and practically. I like the way zooming allows you to go from the small detail to a larger picture, and the other way around. I think what the zoom allows you to do is close to how I myself see the world. I am interested in the small details, and sometimes I feel like I am seated in a corner of the world, observing from a distance, but with a gaze that comes up close.[34]

Moodysson and Brantås both affirm that they had watched *The Killing of a Chinese Bookie* (John Cassavetes, 1976) around the time of filming *Show Me Love*, and Brantås also indicates his fascination for the visual style (including crash zooms) of Hong Kong kung fu movies.[35] Moodysson and film editor Michal Leszczylowski both affirm that Brantås' sensitivity with the camera and his deliberate use of zooms to close-ups helped augment the film's feeling of intimacy and authenticity.[36] Rather than moving the camera to follow the actors, intimacy is achieved through zooms. Similarly, *Show Me Love* mostly eschews panoramas or establishing shots of landscapes, buildings, or other locations; an actor is present in virtually every shot, which helps maintain the focus on the characters and the significance of their story. This strategy, Brantås suggests, shows that the viewer is trusted to make connections and understand the implications of different locations and situations.[37] These cinematographic choices underline the film's strategic ambiguity that blurs the particular and the universal: the camera's focus on Elin and Agnes suggests the characters are isolated individuals whose coming-out story is unique, while the zooms and other close camera work increase the intimacy between the viewer and the actors, helping to create a sense of universal applicability.

Show Me Love, European Film, and Ingmar Bergman

To an international viewer, *Show Me Love* seems to belong to a tradition of 1990s filmmaking in Scandinavia that makes storytelling and acting primary, while relinquishing high production values or fine-tuned visual composition. The Danish Dogme 95 movement helped export this aesthetic as a recognizable mark of European and independent filmmaking in the late 1990s.[38] Another point of comparison would be the first films of the French New Wave, including François Truffaut's 1959 film, *The 400 Blows* (*Les 400 coups*).[39] Like *Show Me Love*, this film was a debut feature, filmed with a portable camera on location, a largely amateur cast, a small crew, and a limited budget. Like Truffaut in *The 400 Blows*, Moodysson focuses on youth while using the surrounding environment to complement the story. Such comparisons with Truffaut come from industry professionals who have been closely involved with Moodysson. They testify to a commonly held perception of Moodysson as a filmmaker in the mold of the European auteur.

Show Me Love's emphasis on two young women follows a Swedish film tradition that takes cinematic depiction of children and youth seriously. The connection was noted by international reviewers who associated the film with some of Sweden's most successful film exports of the 1980s—Lasse Hallström's *My Life as a Dog* (1987) and Ingmar Bergman's *Fanny and Alexander* (1982). *Show Me Love* also nods to what could be called the Pippi Longstocking legacy. Literary narratives about strong, independent girls have been a part of popular Swedish youth culture for decades. Character development and dialogue are central in *Show Me Love*'s screenplay. There is a literary quality to the language, situations, and problems in the film.

In fact, Moodysson published the script to *Show Me Love* shortly after the film's release, like Ingmar Bergman published many of his. In this sense, Moodysson represents a trend in European art film production. Available both in Swedish and in a Danish translation, the printed text of *Fucking Åmål* documents the dialogue spoken in the film and was published in paperback jointly by Memfis and Bokförlaget DN (the publishing company affiliated with *Dagens Nyheter*, Sweden's largest morning newspaper). Alexandra Dahlström, who plays Elin, is featured on the cover; the book also contains a few pictures from the film shoot and a note by Moodysson. It is a highly readable manuscript, the dialogue and scene descriptions combining to create a compelling narrative that stands on its own.

Show Me Love is a classic example of a European auteur film, from Moodysson's close collaboration with a single production company, Memfis, to emphasis on dialogue in his personal storytelling, to his control over screenplay, casting, and scenography, and to his significant input during editing. On the other hand, Moodysson's socially realistic films—*Show Me Love* included—arguably share more similarities with the prominent generation of 1960s and 1970s Swedish filmmakers who rebelled against what they—and the Swedish public at the time—perceived as Bergman's aestheticized and subjective auteur films. These filmmakers include Jan Troell, Stefan Jarl (a strong supporter of Moodysson and his codirector for *The Kids They Sentenced*), and Bo Widerberg who in 1962 penned the manifesto *Visionen i svensk film* (*Vision in Swedish Film*). This treatise calls for increased cinematic (social) realism and opposes Bergman's alleged dominance of the Swedish film industry and abstract, theological, and solipsistic film content.[40]

Moodysson can be seen as a new kind of Swedish auteur. Though Moodysson denies any influence from Swedish director Ingmar Bergman—it is a question brought up repeatedly in interviews—Bergman himself praised *Show Me Love* and called the film "perfect," while recognizing that Moodysson, as he expressed it, "should just keep on making films."[41] With the endorsement of a prominent member of the Swedish film establishment, Moodysson quickly secured auteur status despite his resistance to comparisons with Bergman.[42] And yet, there are intriguing thematic and visual parallels between *Show Me Love* and two of Bergman's internationally best-known and most self-reflexively experimental films, *The Silence* (*Tystnaden*, 1963) and *Persona* (1966). Both of these Bergman films feature complicated and erotically coded relationships between two sisters or otherwise closely connected women, beyond the fact that the protagonists' names in all three films begin with A and E. *Show Me Love*'s evolving relationship between Agnes and Elin bears intriguing resemblances to that of the actress Elisabeth and her nurse Alma in *Persona*. Elisabeth, like Agnes, is coded as quiet (Elisabeth never speaks), reclusive, from a higher class, intellectual, rational, and engaged in introverted artistic practice, while Alma, like Elin, is talkative, spontaneous, working class, sexually experienced, and culturally unsophisticated. Dahlström (Elin) looks almost like a young Bibi Andersson (who plays Alma) — blonde, high cheekbones, striking blue eyes, and a voluptuous mouth. The gender and class codes in *Show Me Love* tie the film to one of Bergman's most acclaimed works.

There is also a striking meta-cinematic gesture to *Persona* in *Show Me Love*. Moodysson includes a shot from a dream sequence that seems to mirror the dream sequence in *Persona*, when Elisabeth and Alma first look at each other's faces as if the camera were a mirror. In a later scene, Elisabeth bends down to seemingly kiss Alma's neck. In *Show Me Love*, Elin has an erotic dream about Agnes. The two young women are shown in a dream sequence in soft focus, tightly blocked in the frame. Their pose recalls one of the most famous shots in *Persona*. Agnes is filmed with her cheek next to Elin's, as in a soft kiss. The dream is not just visually striking but in fact allows us to understand that Elin is sexually attracted to Agnes, just as Agnes is strongly attracted to her. Björklund remarks that Elin tells her sister Jessica upon waking up that she had a bad dream, which suggests "that falling for Agnes is a nightmare to Elin — to be a lesbian is unacceptable in Elin's world."[43] Yet the dream sequence gives Elin's character significant complexity. Within the film's structure, Agnes could be called a stable lesbian, though her utterances counteract such notions of stability. But we know that Moodysson's dialogue is filled with ambivalence: Elin's reference to her eroticized experience as a nightmare is, at this stage, expressed in a sublimated dream form.

Elin (Alexandra Dahlström) dreaming of Agnes (Rebecka Liljeberg) in a scene uncannily reminiscent of a dream sequence in Ingmar Bergman's *Persona*. Frame grab. Image reproduced by permission of Memfis Film.

Persona and *Show Me Love* play with how to cinematically construct an intimacy that is never explicitly sexual but still tinged with erotic desire that appears impossible to perform on screen within the narrative universe of the film. What makes Moodysson's dream sequence remarkable is that it breaks with the bare-basics cinematography that otherwise characterizes *Show Me Love*, in which filters and artificial lighting are largely absent, and the framing and blocking of actors

Elisabeth (Liv Ullman) and Alma (Bibi Andersson) in the famous dream sequence in Ingmar Bergman's *Persona*. Still photography. Image reproduced by permission. *Persona* (c) 1966 AB Svensk Filmindustri.

and faces appears sometimes incidental. Yet, as Brantås remarks, the lighting and mood of this shot were fortuitously authentic: the sun broke through just at the moment they were filming the scene and was filtered through a large pane of translucent glass, which was part of the classroom in which they shot the scene.[44] While Bergman's film is obviously experimental (the opening montage and the break of the film in the middle are just two well-known examples), *Show Me*

Love's challenges to cinematic form and convention are understated and support its strategic implementation of authenticity.

Gwendolyn Audrey Foster indeed argues that *Persona* "is centrally concerned with the performance of lesbian desire" and "challenges the regime of heterosexuality and its norms," while remarking that "much of the literature on *Persona* avoids any discussion of lesbian desire."[45] In *Persona*, Foster argues, "heterosexual sex is almost always associated with abortion and pain." I suggest something similar in *Show Me Love*. The sisters discuss abortion, and Elin initially states that nobody (in this context understood as a man) "will ever insert anything into me," though her first intercourse with Markus is less painful than disappointing. In *Persona*, Foster continues, "Homosexual sex is associated with fear and fascination of the merging of identity . . . as in a shared bond of sisterhood."[46] For Elin, who shares her strongest emotional bond with her sister Jessica, attraction to Agnes can be understood as a threat to an established sense of familial and class belonging. Thus her attraction breaks the already established bond of sisterhood for the possibility of another intimate and explicitly sexual connection, which is threatening in other ways.

Masturbation scenes also connect the three films, in all cases presenting lesbian desire. In *Persona*, Alma tells Elisabeth the story about Katarina and the young boys on the island, in which Katarina's act of masturbation "indirectly consummat[es] their lesbian desire."[47] The infamous masturbation scene in *The Silence* with Ester (Ingrid Thulin) in focus positioned this film as sexually explicit for its US release.[48] The framing of the masturbation scenes in both *Show Me Love* and *The Silence* ends with close-ups on the faces of both actresses. But Moodysson plays with the "gaze" and queers the reference to Bergman.

The Silence focuses on what is suggested as an incestuous relationship between two women who appear to be sisters, Ester and

Anna (Gunnel Lindblom). Moodysson's screenplay for *Show Me Love* originated from a fascination with the two sisters Jessica and Elin, and in subsequent interviews he has stressed how central he perceives the sisters' relationship to be to the film. His fascination with sisterhood also influenced the script of his first short film, *Talk*, about two sisters who are members of a Hare Krishna group. Elin and her sister are in fact intimate; they share a room, the same friends, and are each other's confidantes. Jessica, like Anna in *The Silence*, is the strongest heteronormative force in the film. She tells Elin after she has expressed her initial fascination with the concept of lesbianism that "You are not normal!" Jessica is in fact portrayed as a guardian of both heterosexuality and patriarchy in the film—she does not challenge her boyfriend's abusive ways or her perception that a life in Åmål with Markus is "how it is supposed to be."[49] As Björklund has cogently argued, the world of Jessica and Elin is dominated by male beliefs about women's inferiority, which makes "the girls function as ornaments or decoration more than equal partners of the boys"—though Elin, of course, seeks to rebel.[50]

Persona, *The Silence*, and *Show Me Love* also make striking use of mirror figurations. Foster argues that the scene in *Persona* in which Elisabeth enters Alma's room at night, strokes back her head, and appears to kiss and seduce her (though no sexual activity is represented and the possibility is only suggested) involves "a self-reflexive gaze at the audience" and suggests the viewer identifying with the viewed through a "spectatorial mirror."[51] This is the scene that Moodysson appears to quote in the dream sequence in *Show Me Love*. Mirrors and deep-focus long shots are significant in *The Silence*, as the camera positions Ester and Anna on opposite sides of an ensuite hotel room; confined in a small space in a foreign country, interiors in this film play a critical role in augmenting the tension between the two women. An interesting distinction is how Bergman places that claustrophobia in a foreign locale, in contrast to Moodysson's claustrophobia in a domestic and blandly familiar setting.

By framing Elin through different mirror shots, *Show Me Love* affirms Elin's identity as shifting and dynamic. In contrast, Agnes is rarely figured in a mirror shot. When Elin is getting dressed to go to a party, for example, we see her face in a bathroom mirror as she is applying makeup; this leads to a cut in which Johan is cutting out a photo of her from an old yearbook and hiding it in his wallet, and subsequently to a shot with Agnes looking at Elin's photo. This tightly edited sequence plays on the visual composition of Elin as an object of desire for both Johan and Agnes but quickly turns that convention around. Elin tries to see herself in full figure in the small bathroom mirror but finds that she cannot grasp her own reflection. The shot composition suggests that Elin supersedes the small frame of the mirror in her mother's apartment. Walking out into the hallway in her underwear to use the full-figure mirror in the elevator, Elin and Jessica ride it up and down between the floors while discussing their appearance, with Elin blurting out, "I am so beautiful!" and "I am going to become Miss Sweden." When their mother enters and sees Elin in her underwear, the situation is only partly comic. Elin's shame and frustration is clear, but she is also youthfully defiant at being grounded. "What?!" she says to her mother, "I cannot go to a party because I happen not to wear any pants?" The mother's gaze is a strong affirmation of conventionality. She grounds her daughters, but once she leaves for her night shift, the two head out. The visuals and sequencing here make clear that Elin struggles, as does Agnes, with the idea of fitting in. No mirror can accommodate her full reflection. Her mother and sister do not understand her, and she has yet to find a way to express herself.

Elin (Alexandra Dahlström) finding that the mirror in her mother's small apartment is not large enough to capture her reflection. Another of the film's many symbolic interiors. Frame grab. Image reproduced by permission of Memfis Film.

The parallels and similarities that run throughout *Persona*, *The Silence*, and *Show Me Love* signal the cultural construction of cinematic same-sex desire. This desire is one that can be expressed in meta-cinematic coding, which may or may not be intended or even acknowledged by the filmmaker. That *Show Me Love* was recognized abroad as a lesbian coming-out story much more so than in Sweden may comment both on the international reverberations of Bergman's films about female sexuality and on the perception that Moodysson is taking up the torch of his well-known Swedish predecessor. In contrast to Bergman's characters, who often suffer intense humiliation when challenging sexual conventions (this is striking in both *Persona* and *The Silence*), Moodysson's characters do not.[52] Neither Elin nor Agnes ultimately conforms; their immanent sexual (and social) rebellion is taken seriously as an authentic form of self-expression. The film may apply a number of conventional cinematic and narrative strategies, but its dialogue and aesthetics—including the reverse film stock and sophisticated camera work that plays with the heteronormative cinematic gaze—make it both innovative and original.

Characterization and Casting: Lesbian Intellectual Sophistication vs. Heterosexual Working-Class Popular Culture

Though *Show Me Love* moves between the queer and the heteronormative, the characterization of Agnes is aligned with lesbian cultural markers. Her look is one we are meant to recognize as butch—no makeup, simple hairstyle, baggy pants, and oversized men's shirts. Agnes is an intellectual: she writes poetry and reads Finno-Swedish modernist Edith Södergran (1892–1923). Södergran is understood as one of the first poets writing in the Nordic tradition to allow for the possibility of same-sex desire; her poems, as in the striking "Vierge Moderne" (1916), are formally innovative and thematically ambivalent in terms of the sexual orientation of the speaker and her objects of desire. Södergran's poetry helped spearhead an early and vibrant movement of lyrical modernism in Northern Europe just before the First World War. Agnes echoes the legacy of Södergran. She is construed as an intellectual lesbian poet whose isolation in a small town gives rise to feelings of rebellion as well as of despair. Agnes is part of a stable middle-class context. She has a room of her own, which reflects her interests and gender coding. It contains numerous markers that indicate her as an intellectual and an outsider—the walls are dark blue; posters of Morrissey and classics of Western modern art grace her walls; her CD rack is stocked with eclectic music; from Remo Giazotto's neo-baroque "Albinoni's Adagio in G minor" (1958) to Swedish alternative pop band Broder Daniel. In *Show Me Love*, Agnes' identity as a lesbian is coupled with her intellectual interests. She is silent, serious, and interested in the interiority of human beings—she wants to become either a psychologist or an author. We are thus meant to take her sexual orientation seriously—for her, same-sex desire is not a matter of play-acting. In fact, what Judith Butler famously called the discursive iterative process, a process that continuously reaffirms sexual or gendered identities as if these were naturally given, clearly influences Agnes' characterization. We recognize her as lesbian since her look and behavior appear to reaffirm the discursively constituted markers of lesbian identity.

For many years lesbian identity in the Swedish context has been culturally construed as part of an upper-class or intellectual trajectory, stemming not least from the impact of member of the nobility Agnes von Krusenstjerna's novel series *The Misses von Pahlen* (*Fröknarna von Pahlen*, 1930), contested claims about novelist Selma Lagerlöf's personal life, or later from Louise Boije af Gennäs's novel *Stars Without Vertigo* (*Stjärnor utan svindel*, 1996).[53] Part of the reason that the lesbian aspect of the film was suppressed in Swedish reception, I would argue, is because it did not appear plausible for critics in Sweden that Elin, a working-class young woman with little intellectual or cultural sophistication, could actually be "lesbian." This legacy is different, perhaps, from an American literary tradition that has explored the working-class, butch identity, as exemplified by Leslie Feinberg's *Stone Butch Blues* (1993).[54]

Moodysson's characterization of Elin is ambiguous in this regard—it is not entirely clear whether Elin's character development in the film leads toward lasting identification with lesbianism. Elin's revealing clothes, ample use of makeup, concern with her looks, and less than stellar performance in school appears to affirm cultural coding of her as conventionally heterosexual: this is part of the cultural construction that makes Elin's characterization incongruous. Her family, in contrast to Agnes' stable nuclear family with two professional parents, consists of a single mother who works nights, presumably as a nurse or a nurse's aide. Elin's mother is portrayed as a stereotypical counter-model to heterosexual patriarchy—overweight and unkempt, with a slight trace of dark hair on her lip, she is what could happen when you have two kids without a husband and remain in the boonies. Elin in fact expresses her own worst nightmare as exactly the kind of life and situation her mother occupies. And yet, in contrast to Agnes, who is deeply suspicious of her mother, Elin seeks to confide in hers. She tries the wording out: "Mom, I am a lesbian." But her mother's confused "What?" leads Elin to rephrase her statement affirmatively with "homosexual," and then to recant: "I was only joking." A moment thereafter, Elin asks whether she and her sister really have the same father; her mother responds in the affirmative but closes any further discussion with, "Let's not talk about him now." In these family dynamics, coming out as a lesbian involves a challenge both to sexuality and class.

Show Me Love constructs Elin's and Agnes' sense of feeling confined and circumscribed in terms of interior settings. There are a number of parallel and contrasting scenes in locked rooms and in bathrooms that play on metaphors of inclusion and exclusion. Agnes' home also invokes similar associations to confinement and claustrophobia. Hers may be a middle-class, intellectual home, but Moodysson clearly emphasizes its double standards. As a vegetarian, Agnes is upset at her mother making roast beef for her birthday dinner; upon receiving a bottle of cheap perfume named after the pop singer Robyn as a gift from Viktoria, Agnes' pent-up frustrations erupt. In a gesture typical of *Show Me Love*'s canny manipulation of double registers, Agnes declares angrily, "I cannot accept this." She cannot accept her parents' assumption that she is like any other teenager, that her loneliness and frustration are "normal," and that she enjoys the company of Viktoria. It appears, indeed, as if Agnes wants to be recognized by her family for who she is—a lesbian—but in a scene later in the film we learn how difficult that is for Agnes' mother, who affirms that lesbianism is fine as a concept but refuses to believe that her own daughter could be one. *Show Me Love* shows as well that it knows how the pecking order goes in a youth film of the Hollywood high school type—Agnes' lines directed to Viktoria are cruel. She cannot extend the tolerance she seeks at home to her classmate. In popular youth culture a physical handicap seems worse than anything, a stance which *Show Me Love* reflects. There is an additional layer of psychological metaphor here as well. Viktoria is paralyzed from the waist down; the paralysis in the lower part of her body suggests asexuality. This is perhaps also what increases Agnes' aggression. She does not want to be associated with asexuality. She wants her sexuality taken seriously and for it not to be treated as a form of paralysis.

    The thematic emphasis on group and social dynamics in *Show Me Love* pits the relationship of Elin and Agnes in relief against their peers and against their families. The creative nerve and social relevance of the film depend largely on the principal casting of Dahlström as Elin and Liljeberg as Agnes. But the supporting group of local actors who play their friends also contributes to the film's originality. Moodysson cast Dahlström and Liljeberg from casting calls held at the Memfis production offices in Stockholm, while their peers were selected from local casting calls in Trollhättan. Among the local teenage actors, few had acted before. Moodysson emphasized how he and the production team sought to establish a friendly and open rapport with the young actors, including playing games of floor hockey during the initial casting.[55] The local actors all spoke with a Trollhättan dialect and shared a personal knowledge of attending a small-town high school and the social pressures that it entails.

In contrast, Dahlström and Liljeberg are both from Stockholm and had previous acting experience. Dahlström, fourteen at the time of the film shoot, continued acting in different European productions after *Show Me Love* and is now an award-winning short film director. At the time of the film shoot, she pursued the performance and stage track in her Stockholm high school and had acted professionally in theater productions and youth films. Coming from an intellectual background, she grew up reading Tolstoy, Turgenev, and Dostoyevsky, while expressing strong self-identification with her Russian mother's love of languages, literature, and the arts.[56] Her role as Elin involved emulating not only a different class and educational background but also learning to speak the dialect of the small town of Trollhättan. Elin's regional accent is thick in *Show Me Love*, and Erica Carlson (who plays her sister Jessica) was one of her primary dialogue coaches. As Dahlström states in a research interview, shooting *Show Me Love* was a transformative experience; it brought her unexpected intimacy with a group of Trollhättan adolescents, including Carlson, with whom she may not otherwise have interacted. Liljeberg, two years Dahlström's senior, had also acted previously, including in the television series *Sune's Christmas* (*Sunes jul*, 1991), based on a popular youth novel series, which screened on Swedish television. She pursued acting for a period after *Show Me Love*, including being cast in a small role in Moodysson's *Together*, but she now works as a medical doctor in Stockholm. Her family having moved to the area recently, Agnes is an outsider in the community and hence Liljeberg speaks in her Stockholm dialect throughout the film.

In press interviews the local Trollhättan actors express their excitement at having been part of a film production. Mathias Rust, who plays Johan Hult, relates his desire to become an actor and leave Trollhättan.[57] Dahlström and Liljeberg stem from different intellectual as well as economic classes than their local colleagues; both have continued along these tracks in their careers: Dahlström as an actress and director, Liljeberg as a university-trained physician. Carlson, Rust, and other Trollhättan actors have not maintained acting careers. Hiring Dahlström and Liljeberg, de facto outsiders, was a structural component in the casting of the film that paralleled the fictional premise of Elin and Agnes being different than the local group of teenagers.

Out of the Closet

At the end of the film, Elin quits vacillating, breaks up with Johan by telling him that she is, in fact, in love with somebody else, and appears to have made up her mind about pursuing her own interests. As a sequel to the bridge scene, where Agnes and Elin begin to get to know one another and share a kiss, a similarly symbolic location provides a cathartic setting at the end of the film. Elin grabs Agnes by the arm in the high school hallway and drags her into a small bathroom where she voices her interest in Agnes, even though it remains characteristically conditional: "If you are in love with me, then I am in love with you, too." Her verbal hedging aligns with *Show Me Love*'s consistent refusal to circumscribe Elin's capacity for transformation in conventional cinematic terms. A raucous crowd bangs on the door, led by Elin's posse, who assumes that she has shut herself in the bathroom with a boy. In discussing their trapped situation, Elin is unable to verbalize her thoughts and emotions. Agnes finally takes the lead in a line that bridges the concrete and the metaphorical, the mundane and the existential: "We walk out, of course" (Vi går ut förstås). As they exit, they are featured in close-up against a conspicuously red background of the bathroom's walls; Agnes is slightly in the background, her gaze on Elin. Elin presents her to the crowd, as if it were a stage entrance: "Ta-da! Here I am. This is my new girlfriend." Emerging quite literally from a (water) closet, the young women walk triumphantly hand in hand, smiling through the silently staring crowd, which appears dumbstruck. The camera follows Elin and Agnes closely, and the soundtrack features Broder Daniel's "Underground." The lyrics in this scene underscore the significance of their actions and of reversing a heteronormative gaze: "We look so good, we look so good, we look so good together. / And we are underground, we are underground, we are underground. / And we don't care, we don't care, we don't care what you say about us."[58] Indeed, Elin utters in a defiant voice: "Move over. We're going to go and fuck" (Vi skall gå och knulla). Her statement is celebratory and defiant but also exhibitionistic; it is a version of her sexually confident, "promiscuous" public self. As the two exit the school, the camera follows them in a pan as they leave the schoolyard with sunlight on their faces and wind blowing in their hair.

At the premiere screening in Stockholm, the atmosphere in the

Out of the closet. Agnes (Rebecka Liljeberg) and Elin (Alexandra Dahlström) in the film's penultimate scene. Still photography by Åke Ottoson. Image reproduced by permission of Memfis Film.

cinema was jubilant and ecstatic during this scene, Moodysson recalls in the audio commentary track in a recent Swedish DVD version. This triumphant ending was indeed the final scene in the manuscript, but as the production went on there was a sense within the production team that it did not provide closure. Moodysson added the final improvised scene on the suggestion of line producer Malte Forsell, a gesture characteristic of the small collaborative approach to the production. Moodysson concurs that he quickly realized the power of an epilogue. While the dialogue of the film's final scene was improvised on the set, it ties the film in a circular movement to one of the earliest scenes, in which Elin argues with her sister during breakfast over the last of the cocoa powder. In her closing conversation with Agnes, Elin's lines hover symbolically over a theme of excess and lack; she explains how she has trouble putting the right amount of cocoa powder in her milk, how the glass of milk overflows, and how she puts more and more in. Though a seemingly innocent discussion, the scene operates on a highly productive sense of ambiguity. Indeed, why does Agnes think Elin's story is funny? Is it really unrelated to any kind of seduction or foreplay? Are the girls finding a way to proceed, given their surroundings? Elin exaggerates: "5000 kg of chocolate," while Agnes is constantly looking at Elin, laughing, downing the milk quickly; a pause falls between them. Elin says, "It makes a lot of chocolate milk. But that doesn't matter" (Men det gör ingenting). The implications of her lines are that balance is elusive, that she wants more than what a container can take, and also that Agnes knows exactly what she means and shares her sentiment. In this scene, the young women are finding a way to negotiate their desire for one another: moving toward intimacy that bridges friendship and sexuality.

"The content of the dialogue is not that important," Moodysson states in the DVD commentary, "but the fact that they sit together engaged in conversation is the courageous aspect." Whether the filmmaker acknowledges it or not, this final piece of improvised dialogue about a seemingly ordinary topic has significant implications that are consistent with *Show Me Love*'s thematic and aesthetic strategies. On the surface, the girls discuss a concrete and straightforward issue, but their dialogue signals how they perceive their situation as

Agnes (Rebecka Liljeberg) and Elin (Alexandra Dahlström) in the film's final scene. Still photography by Åke Ottoson. Image reproduced by permission of Memfis Film.

one of lack and excess, as well as their interest in breaking molds and getting more out of life than what their small town would allow with its seemingly stifling conventions. Though Moodysson may be reluctant to express his queering of a traditional romantic climax scene (he notably avoids a voyeuristic sex scene between young women), he infuses the mundane with erotic implications. Elin's expression earlier—that she and Agnes are leaving school early to have sex—is actually continued as a possibility in the final scene of the film. As promised by the film's Swedish title, the young women are possibly about to be "fucking Åmål." But Moodysson leaves the interpretation of this final scene characteristically open.[59] For some viewers, the girls seated on the bed in the final sequence may portray childish innocence rather than prefiguring sexual activity. Similarly, playing Robyn's hit "Show Me Love" during the ending credits may signal a return to the mainstream and heteronormative, as this tune is far from the indie rock of Broder Daniel that Agnes listens to earlier. And yet, the film ends with Agnes looking at Elin in a gesture that seems to be a completion of the first "gaze" in the film and the subsequent journey that gaze takes before reaching this final, intimate scene. The same adoration is present, but the setting has changed. Now the setting has light and privacy. It is quiet. The object of the gaze and the gazer share this space, made available to them at last because of their bold actions. It appears that this "look" fulfills an aesthetic promise that began with the initial queering of the "gaze."

In fact, the light and intimacy of the final scene ties back to Moodysson's interest in interiors and production design as a way to underscore the screenplay's characteristic ambivalence in dialogue and plot development. It is significant that Agnes is being invited to Elin's home to share, at least momentarily, her bed in the room she occupies with her sister. It is also one of few domestic scenes in the film infused with natural sunlight. In contrast to the many darkly lit scenes (thanks to the almost exclusive use of "practicals"), the production design here puts other interior scenes in the film in stark relief—in particular bedrooms and bathrooms. These scenes visualize confinement and effects of social control.[60] With the exception of the final bathroom scene at school, all interior scenes were shot on location. Elin's and Jessica's room, for example, was decorated on the advice of the local Trollhättan actors who played Elin's friends. They helped choose the pinkish wall color and the posters on the wall. They also wrote the notes pinned on it. As Moodysson recalls, their involvement was critical to the feeling of authenticity he wanted actress Dahlström to experience—indeed, some of the young women even had a sleepover on the set to further immerse themselves in their roles. Agnes' room, on the other hand, was more closely monitored by Moodysson in collaboration with scenographer Lina Strand. Moodysson was involved even in minute details of this stage set that are not discernible in the film, including the order in which the CDs were lined up in the rack next to the stereo. Similarly, the posters on the wall were vetted by Moodysson, and some of the children's drawings pinned on it came directly from Moodysson's own children.[61] It is clear from interviews and the DVD commentary track that Moodysson understood the scenography and production design to be critical to the authenticity and realism he was interested in cultivating. The production design, dialogue, camera work, and lighting in this final scene all operate on multiple, distinct levels; as a whole, *Show Me Love* affirms a queer trajectory. Its characters literally come out of the closet and explore their mutual desire.

New Queer Cinema and the Hollywood High School Film

In terms of genre and film history, *Show Me Love* reflects and deconstructs several established generic trajectories in Swedish, Hollywood, and European cinema. As Harry Benshoff and Sean Griffin claim, historically films made "outside Hollywood often had a more complex take on human sexuality. For example, the first film ever to feature homosexual love as its theme may have been the Swedish film *Wings*

(*Vingarne*, 1916), directed by Mauritz Stiller."[62] Successful exports of Swedish film from the 1950s onward, particularly Arne Mattson's *One Summer of Happiness* (*Hon dansade en sommar*, 1951), Ingmar Bergman's *Summer with Monika* (*Sommaren med Monika*, 1953), and Vilgot Sjöman's *I Am Curious Yellow* (*Jag är nyfiken gul*, 1967), in combination with liberal pornography laws and a straightforward cultural approach to (hetero)sexual practices, helped to brand Sweden and Swedish film abroad as sexually explicit. Significant counterparts among European films about young women that feature implicit or explicit erotic same-sex attraction include Diane Kurys's *Peppermint Soda* (*Diabolo menthe*, 1977) and *Coup de foudre* (1983), as well as Chantal Akerman's *Je, tu, il, elle* (1977). But *Show Me Love* takes the lesbian coming-of-age and coming-out story away from the realm of the spectacular—there are no vampires, no Paris by night, and no wildly experimental elements in the film—and introduces lesbian desire as a significant aspect of everyday youth culture.

Show Me Love is also significant in the development of an international queer cinema in the 1990s for reasons concerning distribution and its reception—it was widely screened and won awards not just in Scandinavia but all over the world. In this sense, *Show Me Love* reflects an alternate film landscape in the wake of what film critic Ruby Rich calls the "New Queer Cinema" of the early 1990s. This wave has been closely identified with North American independent films of critical acclaim, including Jennie Livingstone's *Paris is Burning* (1990), Todd Haynes' *Poison* (1991), Tom Kalin's *Swoon* (1992), and Gus Van Sant's *My Own Private Idaho* (1991). But the wave also includes European counterparts like the Dutch *Antonia* by director Marleen Gorris (1995) and many of Spanish filmmaker Pedro Almodóvar's films from the 1990s, including *All About My Mother* (*Todo sobre mi madre*, 1999). Though the films of New Queer Cinema are heterogeneous and disparate in form as well as content, they share, in Ruby Rich's words, "an attitude"; the films are "energetic" and what J. Hoberman of the *Village Voice* calls "proudly assertive."[63] In fact, Michele Aaron traces a certain "defiance" in these films.[64] It is important to keep in mind, however, that before the 1990s, lesbians on screen in popular film, especially in mainstream American cinema, tended to be portrayed as stalkers, psychotics, vampires, murderers, alcoholics, or anonymous sidekicks, as represented in mainstream films like *A Walk on the Wild Side* (Edward Dmytryk, 1962), *Vampire Lovers* (Roy Ward Baker, 1970), *The Hunger* (Tony Scott, 1983), or *Basic Instinct* (Paul Verhoeven, 1992).[65] These films operate on figurations of the debased or doomed lesbian, for whom death is a likely outcome. Though *Show Me Love* departs from such character and plot figurations, Agnes, attempted suicide does potentially seem like one place where the film engages the "doomed lesbian" formula of earlier cinema representations that results in suicide or premature death as punishment (especially under the Hollywood Production Code from 1934 to the early 1960s). After this brief episode, the film abruptly changes direction and no one dies.

Around the time that *Show Me Love* was conceived, "feel-good" Hollywood-style movies with happy endings for same-sex protagonists were becoming more prevalent. In fact, Aaron lists *Show Me Love* among a group of films that relinquish their "radical impulse" in order to cater to a "niche market" and are, therefore, "innocuous and often unremarkable"; for Björklund it "fulfills most of the genre expectations of the romantic comedy," though she also claims that the film "challenges and queers the genre."[66]

Show Me Love is thereby a cousin to several contemporary independent US queer films with young protagonists, such as *The Incred-*

ibly True Adventure of Two Girls in Love (Maria Maggenti, 1995), *Beautiful Thing* (Hettie Macdonald, 1996*)*, *Edge of Seventeen* (David Moreton, 1998), and *Billy's Hollywood Screen Kiss* (Tommy O'Haver, 1998). These films constitute a subgenre of queer youth films, a development of gay and lesbian cinema at the end of the 1990s. The high school setting provides a cultural baseline for films like *The Incredibly True Adventure of Two Girls in Love* and *Edge of Seventeen*. It emphasizes both the generic quality of youth experience in the United States, Europe, and Sweden, as well as the effort it takes to break free from social and cultural constraints. But *Show Me Love* takes the norms of this subgenre and queers them. Although *Show Me Love* may be typical of what Michael Bronski has called "the positive image" politics of coming-out films, which construct a "triumphant, individualist narrative arc" that also "misjudges the harshness of homophobia in the world," Moodysson's film, Bronski continues, actually "radically challenges" the genre as it posits "lesbianism as a simple fact."[67] Moodysson's film partakes in the cultural project of making a lesbian coming-out story into something that can, for the first time in Swedish film history, be visually enacted on the screen. The film's ambivalence toward its protagonists and its status as a landmark of gay and lesbian film make it possible to understand the film as deconstructing boundaries between straight and queer culture at the end of the 1990s. One of the primary vehicles for doing this involves the film's focus on the high school setting in which social pressure and stigmatization often preclude the realization of queer attraction. The high school setting shows that lesbian love in a mainstream or everyday context continues to be problematic and fraught with tension. The seemingly upbeat ending with the possible reading of Agnes and Elin finding themselves in a paradigm of conventional heteronormativity further situates *Show Me Love* as a film that reflects prevailing trends of 1980s and 1990s Hollywood youth film.

In fact, *Show Me Love* draws quite explicitly on characteristics of the American teen movie genre. The unifying location for these films is the high school—many also involve the plot turn of the house party, as does *Show Me Love*—and the restrictions and social pressures that this setting makes visible. Films aimed at and featuring teens reemerged as profitable vehicles for the American movie industry by the 1980s, arguably as a reaction against the preceding decade's emphasis on serious or more adult-oriented fare. Film scholar Timothy Shary shows how "the conspicuous resurgence of teen films in the 1980s" can be traced to the popularity of MTV from its debut in 1981 to low-budget slasher films of the early '80s—*Halloween* (John Carpenter, 1978), *Friday the 13th* (Sean Cunningham, 1980), and *A Nightmare on Elm Street* (Wes Craven, 1984), among others. Shary also points to an increasingly candid portrayal of teenage sexual quests in films like *Risky Business* (Paul Brickman, 1983) and *Fast Times at Ridgemont High* (Amy Heckerling, 1982).[68]

Though less accepting toward or explicit about teen sex, the quintessential high school and teen films by director and writer John Hughes (*Sixteen Candles*, 1984; *The Breakfast Club*, 1985; *Pretty in Pink*, 1986; and *Some Kind of Wonderful*, 1987) portrayed their characters as complex individuals with competing motives. Most of the 1980s teen films were unequivocally heterosexual. As Jeffrey P. Dennis's comprehensive review of teen films reveals, US popular youth culture during the 1980s and 1990s was intensely heteronormative—there simply were no examples of gay or lesbian everyday youth life in mainstream Hollywood cinema or television during these decades.[69] Dennis notes in particular that the male Brat Pack casts were "amazingly homogenous, all masculine, [white,] athletic, attractive, ... heterosexual (not one publicly gay and very few subject of gay rumours)."[70]

Moodysson affirms that he found Hollywood youth films of the 1980s and early 1990s intriguing and fascinating, although he refrains from pointing out any as a particular source of inspiration or as having had an impact on *Show Me Love*. Anything but a conventional Hollywood high school film, Larry Clark's sexually explicit *Kids* (1995) did make a strong impression, however. In terms of other youth films, Moodysson mentions Swedish art film director Roy Andersson's *A Love Story* (*En kärlekshistoria*, 1970) and indicates how to him this film captured "a sense of life, of what it is like to be young, sensations of newness and openness, of the everyday being magic, and how different experiences of a similar situation may be to different people. I remember that film as beautifully capturing the light and the environment, and also that I wanted *Show Me Love* to be harder, more fragmented."[71] *Show Me Love* builds on a Swedish and Scandinavian film tradition of quality youth films, but it is also conceived with clear references to the Hollywood high school and American youth film. This is clear in its thematic emphasis on gendered social conformity and hierarchical group pressure, which in *Show Me Love* is also aesthetically reflected by the emphasis on confinement.

As in Hollywood youth films of the 1980s and early 1990s, *Show Me Love*'s complementary characters are crucial in establishing a baseline heteronormative ideology. Elin's sister Jessica and her boyfriend Markus, his friend Johan (who has a crush on Elin and with whom Elin has a brief relationship), and Agnes' disabled classmate Viktoria provide the background against which Elin and Agnes' actions are projected. In the second half of the film, the constellation of Jessica/Markus and Elin/Johan foreground the stifling gender conventions that are part of the social and cultural framework that *Show Me Love* both criticizes and portrays as authentic and realistic.

There are two critical scenes that show these four characters together. In the first, we encounter each couple seated on a park bench near a playground as they discuss their plans for the future. They are positioned against bare trees and an overcast sky; the light is grey and diffused. The young men are on an educational track leading to trade school in order to become mechanics or electricians. Jessica hopes to study cosmetology or hair styling but concedes that her low grades make a leisure studies track more likely. Elin suddenly breaks the mold. Channeling Agnes, she states that she wants to become a psychologist. She faces immediate objections, and Markus ridicules her aspirations. The composition of this scene is striking. The camera frames each couple closely, intercutting between each as the discussion moves back and forth. Then suddenly the camera zooms out and we see that the two couples are seated apart from each other with a distance of about twenty feet between them. The close association first established between the couples, as if they are completely alike, is broken filmically and in terms of content as Elin asserts her right to wish for something more than the vocational high school track she has until now accepted as a given. Markus' and Jessica's comments make clear that that they believe Elin may be pretty but not smart. With Elin at the far right of the screen, the chasm between her and her sister (at the far left) becomes visually obvious. A significant distance separates them, metaphorically and concretely, in this shot. Once the camera zooms out, we also see that the four characters are seated next to a deserted playground. An empty sandbox contributes to the positioning of these four adolescents as halfway between children and adults. The setting of this scene also demonstrates Moodysson's canny use of authentic social milieus to reveal the immanence

Markus (Stefan Hörberg) and Erica (Jessica Olsson) discussing their future. Still photography by Åke Ottoson. Image reproduced by permission of Memfis Film.

of class and gender status: While these characters may be products of a social welfare state whose policies advocate gender and class equality, these adolescents' trajectories in life were established long ago. Any challenge to the norm, as in the case of Elin's rebellion, is a threat.

The next scene with these two couples exposes this deepening rupture between Elin and her peers. Elin's emerging understanding of gender inequality helps propel her move toward Agnes and the values associated with Agnes' intellectual and middle-class upbringing.

A widening gap between Elin (Alexandra Dahlström) and her sister Erica (Jessica Olsson). Frame grab. Image reproduced by permission of Memfis Film.

This underscores what appears to be an underlying premise of *Show Me Love*, namely that lesbian desire is barred from a working-class context; it is the privilege of the bourgeoisie.

In keeping with the limitations of the Hollywood high school film, as Elin's desire cannot be incorporated into the social homogeneity of her peer group, she is required to relinquish her working-class background. This framework becomes explicit in the second scene in which the two young heterosexual couples are shown together. On Saturday night, just after Elin and Johan become a couple, they watch the entertainment program *Bingolotto* together on television at Elin's home. This bingo show was a staple of Swedish television for more than a decade. Led by a folksy host and featuring low-brow *Schlager* or dance band performances, *Bingolotto* was strongly associated with working-class audiences. As they watch this show, Markus and Johan discuss cell phones. Markus offers the observation that girls really know nothing about technology and are better at other things. Elin challenges him on what exactly this gender difference might entail, and Markus replies that women know about makeup, hair, and how to make themselves pretty. Turning to Johan for his opinion, and receiving answers that appear to support Markus' view, Elin promptly walks into another room, calls the cell phone from her land line, and breaks up with Johan, asking him to leave immediately. This scene—shot to emphasize the claustrophobia of *Show Me Love*'s interiors—formulates Elin's growing awareness of her background, including its gender and class codes. Elin recognizes the problems and contradictions in the social paradigm, but she cannot verbally express what it is that she objects to. Instead, she abruptly and decisively breaks off the relationship with Johan. This action incurs her sister's ire and frustration. The film shows that Elin's interest in Agnes and the life and options associated with her character mean a break with her own background and her close relationship with her sister. Elin cannot name her frustration, but she can act it out. Her actions, in this sense, reflect Moodysson's understanding of his own film as ambiguous: It presents the possibility of lesbian attraction, but Moodysson declines to define the film as a lesbian love story.

In fact, this breakup scene is consistent with most other episodes featuring Elin in her home. At home, she cannot voice what she wants or thinks; she is infantilized, as evidenced, for example, in the film's initial quarrel about chocolate milk. The sexism of contemporary

Swedish society is depicted as implicit and normal in *Show Me Love*. It is neither violent nor obviously contested, but it is clear that it is absolutely deadening. Jessica upholds her connection to Markus but cannot express why. She refers vaguely to a notion that the two were meant to be together. She quite plausibly chooses the less macho Johan at the end of the film, but the values and approaches to life remain similar with both young men. This implicit critique of gender roles is one of the most striking aspects of *Show Me Love* and helps situate the film as at least partly subversive and as part of New Queer Cinema.

Conclusion

Show Me Love is Sweden's first lesbian coming-of-age and coming-out film. It at once bridges categories and deconstructs them. *Show Me Love* also helped put the small town on the map as a cinematic location, and its production far from the established film industry in Stockholm made it a primary example of the regionalization of the film industry in Sweden and elsewhere in Europe around the turn of the millennium. The emphasis Moodysson puts on questions of authenticity and realism in numerous commentaries is significant. As a way of concluding this chapter, I want to present a story that perhaps appears to validate the director's interest in authenticity and realism. After having finished the film, one member of the film team, as Moodysson recalls it,

> put me in touch with a young woman from Åmål, whose story seemed to echo that of my screenplay. I wanted her to read the script and we subsequently met at a cafe in Göteborg to talk about it. I was very nervous about what she would think, but I remember she

said she liked it. And the similarities were uncanny. She had indeed come out as a lesbian in Åmål, there had been a party where people had said they would show up, she had had a short relationship with a girl from the cool clique, school mates had scribbled graffiti on her locker in high school (as some of the students do on Agnes' in *Show Me Love*), and indeed, there were several other parallels. She said Åmål was an awful place and as soon as she turned 18, she left for the big city. This was a validating experience for me. The screenplay was of course completely finished by the time I heard her story, yet it felt like the fact that she was from *Åmål*, not just any town, was very significant, perhaps even magical.[73]

Offset against the end of a decade that saw an increasing fascination with sexual identity construction and enactment, *Show Me Love*'s small-town setting initially appears counterintuitive. On the one hand, as Björklund suggests, Elin and Agnes queer the small-town as the film insists on situating their coming-out story in tension with their attempted escape to Stockholm. But *Show Me Love* operates in double registers in this regard as well. In the depiction of sexuality, genre affiliation, visual aesthetics, dialogue, and characterization, the tension between small-town life and imagined liberation in the big city reflects the oscillation between the radical and the conventional, the mundane and the unusual. If *Show Me Love* breaks down barriers between queer and straight cinema, it also helps to shatter stereotypical cinematic representations of the Swedish small town and exemplifies the regionalization and decentralization of Swedish film production since the mid-1990s. I turn to the implications of these trends in the next chapter.

Show Me Love makes manifest Moodysson's interest in authenticity. As he expresses in numerous interviews, and as echoed by a number of people who have worked closely with him, Moodysson wants his films to appear honest and true. His films thus are representative of a stronghold in Swedish filmmaking that emphasizes social realism but also indicate an intriguing fluidity in concepts like authenticity and verisimilitude. In fact, this film (and Moodysson's oeuvre in general) experiments with the notion that authentic experience is ambiguous. For Moodysson, "truthfully" representing the conflicted lives of young women involves no contradiction in terms despite the fact that he, the producer Jönsson, and the film's A-list crew were all older men. Moodysson appears to assume that film can make evident and credible those intellectual and emotional processes that transcend age, gender, class, and sexuality. His role as filmmaker is to access these thoughts and emotions and to render them into frames. As such, *Show Me Love* attests to his agency as a practitioner precisely in this regard.

3
The Geography of *Show Me Love*

This chapter discusses *Show Me Love*'s international reception, landscape and location depiction, and production and funding parameters. It argues that the film both reflects and helps produce geographical and spatial complexities that the seemingly stable, small, and self-sufficient state of Sweden encountered at the end of the twentieth century. From this perspective, *Show Me Love* appears to be a nostalgic, cinematic reverie of small-town life at a time when few small towns were considered as worthy screen locations. For decades they had remained outside the scope of popularly received Swedish films. Local elements are significant in the film's production history—it is the first feature film shot exclusively in the small Swedish town of Trollhättan, where the new film production center Film i Väst is located. *Show Me Love*'s domestic and international success gave credence to this production center as "Trollywood" and helped it rise to domestic and international prominence—over 250 films have since been coproduced by Film i Väst.

Show Me Love's production history also illustrates a historical moment when Sweden became increasingly denationalized culturally and politically. Sweden's entry into the European Union in 1995 led to partial decentralization of cultural and economic policy. These changes correlate with increasing political and popular recognition that by the mid-1990s Sweden had become a fully multiethnic country thanks to large-scale immigration. Sweden of course also receives a substantial amount of its popular culture from international sources, Hollywood and the US entertainment industry included.[1] *Show Me Love*, as I show more specifically later in this chapter, is the first mainstream product that made the European Union visible in Swedish popular culture. It thereby exemplifies and illustrates the complex renegotiation process of the nation-state at the end of the 1990s. Shunning extensive landscape depiction, *Show Me Love* appears in this formal respect to negate the traditional significance of nature imagery for Swedish national identity and Swedish film. A study of *Show Me Love*'s geography, including its international reception, landscape depiction, and production history, foregrounds a complex cultural construction of Sweden and Europe at the end of the twentieth century.

International Reception and Assumptions about "Swedishness"

The international reception of *Show Me Love* indicates how this film bridges the local and the global, particularly as it became known internationally as a queer film classic, but also in ways that illustrate how geographical tensions within it challenge assumptions about its "Swedishness" as perceived from abroad. *Show Me Love* premiered in Sweden in October 1998 and has since been distributed to over thirty countries, extending in geographical reach from the Nordic countries to many in Europe (including Estonia, France, Italy, the

Netherlands, Russia, Slovakia, Spain, and the UK), Australasia (including Australia, Korea, Japan, New Zealand, and Singapore), and the Americas (including Argentina, Canada, Colombia, Puerto Rico, and the US).[2] The film had its international debut at the Berlin Film Festival in February 1999, where it won a Teddy award for best feature film with gay and lesbian content. At the Karlovy Vary Film Festival, the film earned two awards. In March and April 1999, *Show Me Love* premiered in Denmark, Norway, and Finland, where it was generally warmly received.[3] Moodysson won a Norwegian Amanda award for best foreign film; the film was also nominated for a Danish Bodil award for best non-American film. In the United Kingdom, *Show Me Love* received recognition in 1999 as a British Film Institute Sutherland Trophy—Special Mention and was positively reviewed in *The Independent*, *The Observer*, and *The Scotsman*, among others.[4] French and German coverage included reviews and interviews with Moodysson in newspapers such as *Le Monde* and *Frankfurter Allgemeine Zeitung* and magazines like *Der Spiegel* and *Die Welt*.[5]

In North America, *Show Me Love* received an especially strong welcome in Canada, where it screened both at the Montreal Film Festival and at the Toronto Film Festival in the fall of 1999. In general, Canadian press reviews—like those from Australia—were very favorable,[6] while journalists in the United States were slightly less forthcoming. The *New York Times* acknowledgd that the film, which screened in distribution in New York City and Los Angeles, "has some charm, but not one iota of depth" (Gates), while *Newsweek*'s short presentation highlighted what it described as the film's "honesty, charm," and "uncanny sympathy for all its characters" (Ansen).[7] Despite its small budget, seemingly marginal setting, dialogue in Swedish, generally unknown actors, and a rookie director, *Show Me Love* had significant international reach in mainstream venues, which testifies to the fact that the film was perceived as significant by and for broad audiences in many countries.[8]

The selection of *Show Me Love* for multiple international gay and lesbian film festivals indicates that the film was quickly understood internationally as part of a particular genre in terms of audience appeal. A review of international press about the film reveals less hesitation about describing the film as a lesbian romance and coming-out story than was initially the case for most Swedish reviewers.[9] *Show Me Love*'s international reviewers tend to situate the film as part of an established genre of Hollywood-esque teen and high school films to a much higher extent than do Swedish reviewers. The international press also highlights that although the plot may put a (lesbian) spin on formulaic Hollywood representations of teen romance and youth angst, the film remains sympathetic, authentic, and heartfelt. Though perhaps not immediately apparent to international reviewers, *Show Me Love*'s challenge to Swedish and Nordic film conventions stems more from its portrayal of romance between women and less from its apparently realistic portrayal of youth culture—candid films about adolescence are plentiful in the Swedish tradition and include Lasse Hallström's Oscar-winning *My Life as a Dog* (*Mitt liv som hund*, 1987).[10]

A review in the London paper *The Independent* exemplifies the stance of many international comments: "Contrary to appearances, America isn't the only country making movies about teen love in high school," and though "*Show Me Love* hasn't the polish of its hipper American counterparts it has something far more important, and that's a heart."[11] Tokyo's *The Daily Yomiuri* calls it a "high school classic, and it is not to be missed."[12] According to *The Observer*, *Show Me Love* is "the most engaging film to have emerged from Sweden for some while," while other commentators relate Moodysson to the most famous of his Swedish predecessors.[13] Canada's *The Globe and Mail* suggests the director's last name as "Bergmanesque" in its suggestion of moody emotional spleen, while Montreal's *The Gazette* contrasts the blockbuster appeal of *Show Me Love* in Sweden as markedly different from the reception of most of Bergman's films in his native country.[14]

A number of reviews tout the fact that *Show Me Love* nearly outdid James Cameron's *Titanic* (1997) at the Swedish box office.[15] Others relate the film to a documentary tradition strong in Scandinavian film history.[16] Some detect parallels with Dogme 95 filmmaking.[17] Teenage torment becomes even more gripping and authentic in the documentary-like portrayal of Sweden, where despite the country's image of sexual liberalism and well-known policies of social gender equality, it is still difficult to come out as a lesbian.[18] These connections relate to long-established perceptions of Swedish political and sexual liberalism as being part of the country's perceived distinctiveness in the context of popular culture. Cultural stereotypes of Swedish sin, sex, and suicides (not least in cinematic representation) in place since the 1950s—and exported through many Bergman films in the 1960s—continue to remain significant contextual markers.[19] In fact, a number of reviewers seem nostalgically to pitch a notion of Swedish-style authenticity in opposition to Hollywood fantasy and distortion. *Show Me Love* thus seems to reflect for international viewers an established view of Swedish culture in tune with authentic expressions of female sexuality, albeit tormented. *Show Me Love* perpetuates this stereotype but also modifies it because it portrays female *homo*sexuality.

The English title, *Show Me Love*, suggests that Lukas Moodysson's first feature film is a generic youth romance. This title supports an interpretation of the film as a conventional coming-of-age story that ascribes to the Western heteronormative cultural hegemony and the prescriptions of Hollywood teen films. At the same time, the English title masks the subversive lesbian romance, which challenges genre categorization and helps deconstruct borders between straight and queer cinema.

The film's Swedish title, *Fucking Åmål*, offers up other venues of interpretation. "Åmål" is not a human character but a generic small town in Sweden. It is a typical town name in jokes that emphasize provinciality. Indeed, the film looks like it could be set anywhere in contemporary northwestern Europe—the apartment buildings, the standard highway overpass, and the nondescript school are completely anonymous. Similarly, as critics and audiences have emphasized, its story and plot appear compellingly "universal"—or at least Western—and thus largely decoupled from a specific location or origin. The juxtaposition of "Fucking" and "Åmål" in the title, however, bridges the locally Swedish (the town of Åmål and its cultural allusions in a national context) and the international reach of English: the word "fucking" is used liberally in contemporary informal Swedish as an amplifier (both positive and negative). The title in Swedish and its transformation into English is indicative of globalizing gestures— the Swedish emphasizes an association with World English; in translation it becomes generic Hollywoodese. Like its title, the film's production parameters and international reception span a number of spatial registers. One such register involves a paradox: Though the title in Swedish is geographically specific, the film includes limited landscape depiction and, indeed, was not even shot in the small town for which it is named. In this sense, *Show Me Love* is actually a perfect case study for studying the geographical complexity of contemporary popular culture. This film is simultaneously place-specific and delocalized, thus lending itself to analysis from a number of specific spatial vantage points that raise questions about what is local and global, national and regional, state-related and supra-state initiated, or genuine and fabricated. Several reviewers briefly note the transformation of the film's title from an explicit sexual reference to the generic *Show Me Love* in English-speaking countries and to *Raus aus Åmål* (literally, "leaving Åmål") in German-speaking areas (the original title has been maintained in several languages, including French). Commentators explain that the original title refers to a small town in Sweden, which suggests that the provincial setting of *Show Me Love* actually maintains significance in an international context—the characters Elin and Agnes do not just live in some anonymous small town but in a town that has a name and specific context deserving of explanation despite descriptions that call it "faceless" or a "nowhere town."[20] This may seem like a small point, but it has provoked discussions of Moodysson's representation of location. As Philip French from *The Observer* notes, Moodysson has chosen Åmål "for its proverbial vacuity" and has gone "out of his way to rob the place of any beauty of character," rendering it "claustrophobically uninviting."[21] The setting appears realistic and authentic to reviewers who may have little personal experience of Sweden, which was certainly part of what Moodysson wanted to achieve in his location and landscape depiction.

Location vs. Landscape: Representing Åmål and the Legacy of Swedish Cinematic Countryside

Place representation in *Show Me Love* contrasts both with a legacy of landscape beauty that has been a prominent feature of Swedish and Scandinavian film for many decades and the historical centrality of Stockholm as a film production and film policy center. It includes several scenes set at the bridge leading over the highway to Stockholm. Underlit and shot at night, these scenes lack the distinctive luminescence often attributed to films made in Scandinavia. They make the surroundings appear as a backdrop of utter depression and complete anonymity. The bridge is a charged metaphorical site for what can be seen as Elin's "crossing over" to an interest in Agnes' alternative life (trajectory) and sexual identity. Elin is the one who flags a car for their professed hitchhike to Stockholm, and this act appears to be her first realization that she, also, could eventually leave her hometown and begin another life.[22] The pivotal bridge scene of *Show Me Love* also contrasts with images of wild, natural, and pristine landscapes that Scandinavian cinema have helped construct and market as an integral aspect of high-quality films. As scholars have argued, this tradition has been particularly prominent in the history of Swedish film.

Striking landscape depiction and on-location shooting were critical to the internationally perceived distinctiveness of Swedish silent cinema, including such golden-age classics as Victor Sjöström's *The Outlaw and His Wife* (*Berg-Ejvind och hans hustru*, 1918) and Mauritz Stiller's *Sir Arne's Treasure* (*Herr Arnes pengar*, 1919).[23] Erik Hedling succinctly summarizes the significance of an aestheticized natural landscape in Swedish film history—a trend that marks a certain continuity of the popular artistic representations of landscape by the 1890s group of national romantic painters, including Anders Zorn and Carl Larsson. Erik Hedling suggests that by the 1930s the portrayal of landscapes in Swedish cinema was less about nostalgic reminiscing on a national past and more about promoting a progressive national identity in line with the emerging welfare state. In this way, Hedling argues, depicting nature also meant "celebrating modernity, social change, heritage, and tradition while politically preparing audiences for the emergence of the modern and very urban social democratic welfare state. . . . Landscape, in fact, became a firmly encoded metaphor for the high values of Swedish-ness."[24] Since then Swedish cinematic landscape depiction has come to signify national purity, cohesion, and a shared historical background.[25]

Show Me Love contributes to Swedish cinema first by refusing extended landscape or location shots and second by not aestheticizing the limited depiction of its provincial setting. The film contains no captivating vistas or attempts to make any of its locations appear beautiful, just as it refuses to aestheticize or sexualize the relationship between Elin and Agnes. In *Show Me Love*, there is no link between the Swedish landscape and the figure of a Swedish woman; there is in fact no connection between sexual exploration and the natural landscape, which, of course, provided a selling factor of some of Sweden's most notorious international hits—for example, Arne Mattson's *One Summer of Happiness* (*Hon dansade en sommar*, 1951) and Ingmar Bergman's *Summer with Monika* (*Sommaren med Monika*, 1953). Moodysson's refusal to aesthetically or sexually fetishize the provincial posits *Show Me Love* in contrast to an established practice of landscape and location depiction in Swedish and Nordic film.

In *Show Me Love*, the alienation experienced by the main characters is correlated with the mundane locations in which the two young women are situated. A parallel rejection of aesthetically enhanced nature is emphasized in some of the first Dogme 95 films, Vinterberg's *The Celebration* (*Festen*, 1998) and von Trier's *The Idiots* (*Idioterne*, 1998). The Dogme 95 manifesto stipulates that filming must be on-location and prohibits the use of filters or other tools to augment visual quality. Indeed, the introductory shaky shots of the Danish rural countryside in *The Celebration* can be seen as effectively destabilizing the long tradition of landscape portrayal in Scandinavian cinema; the suburban locations in *The Idiots* are upscale but resolutely mundane and reflect the film's thematic insistence on the pretension and falsehood of the Danish middle class. *Show Me Love*'s insistence on capturing the mundane locations of a small town, such as a highway bridge, a children's playground, or a hockey rink, can also be understood as a part of 1990s criticism of European art film, auteur cinema, and the European heritage film tradition.

As Erik Hedling has argued, *Show Me Love* is set against "a backdrop of drab landscapes and extremely ugly 1960s city-scapes," which thereby makes it also representative of landscape construction in "post-utopian European cinema."[26] Hedling's comments on *Show Me Love* appear in an article devoted to depictions of the Swedish landscape and welfare state in two of Ingmar Bergman's internationally best-known films, *Winter Light* (*Nattvardsgästerna*, 1963) and *Persona* (1966). Moodysson seemingly rejects the wondrously stark landscape in Bergman's *Persona*, shot on Fårö Island in the Baltic Sea, in which striking nature shots offset the intensifying relation of the two main female characters. Shots in *Persona* appear as images of high aesthetic value and as staged fashion shots set against a natural landscape. They are high in contrast, in geometric lines, in crisp shades, and in deep focus. The women emerge as aestheticized icons against that backdrop. *Show Me Love* also resists treating nature or the features of natural light as sources of a (troubled) spiritual or metaphysical connection, as Bergman does in *Through a Glass Darkly* (*Såsom i en spegel*, 1961) or *Winter Light*. Yet there are connections between Moodysson and Bergman in terms of their fascination for their respective filming locations. Moodysson has expressed in a number of interviews how important he finds the environment of Trollhättan. Similarly for Bergman, the Fårö landscape seems to have been singularly expressive. As he notes in an interview: "I just felt that it was my landscape."[27] Yet, as Birgitta Steene argues, Bergman's use of the Fårö landscape "broke the last ties with the glittering and melodramatic summer landscapes of Swedish cinema."[28] Though Bergman's films have not generally been interpreted as critiques of the Swedish welfare state, their landscapes may indeed point that way.[29]

But the legacy of Swedish and Scandinavian cinematic "glittering and melodramatic summer landscapes" has remained a significant component of the wave of (relatively) internationally successful and (relatively) big-budget Scandinavian heritage films from the 1980s and early 1990s—Gabriel Axel's *Babette's Feast* (*Babettes gæstebud*, 1988) and Jan Troell's *Hamsun* (1996) included.[30] The aestheticized landscapes in these films combine with what appears to be a nostalgic attachment to the past in Scandinavian and Swedish culture—trends which *Show Me Love* seems to debunk. Similar trends were strong in contemporary European film. Nature and landscape representation in the European heritage films of the 1990s, Rosalind Galt argues, helped gloss over depictions of both contemporary and historical political and social problems. While the heritage film genre "depends on the production of a beautiful landscape," it promotes "a homogenized prettiness that lacks any genuine engagement with place."[31] Seen from this perspective, *Show Me Love*'s emphasis on the contemporary moment precludes any obviously crafted landscape. On the other hand, *Show Me Love*'s emphasis on the small town, both on screen and in the title, marked a new understanding of place and location in Swedish film production practices and cinematic spatial representations at the end of the 1990s.

Show Me Love helped shape a recognizable new provincial landscape aesthetic, as part of a group of films shot near new regional production centers during the period from 1998 to 2005. Rather than sweeping location shots of nature expanses or a backlit close-up of a raindrop on a birch leaf, these films include 1960s apartment buildings, fast food or pizza joints, rusty cars or idle farming equipment, silos, and industrial storage space—overcast skies lending everything a tone of gray.[32]

This aesthetic representation of provincial landscapes tends to deemphasize the spectacular or unique. Employing fairly conventional narratives, many of these films revolve around a number of easily recognized stereotypes that emphasize (with some exceptions) the small town and the provincial countryside as the site of a deindustrialized, impoverished, and uneducated working class that is also ethnically homogeneous, patriarchal, and heteronormative. A driving plot motivator in these films involves pitching the big city visitor/returnee against the culturally backward hometown residents, often for laughs, as in Josef Fares' *Kopps!* (2003), or for melodramatic effects, as in Maria Blom's *Dalecarlians (Masjävlar,* 2004).[33] The provincial denizen is systematically othered in these films. He or she emerges as unsophisticated. He or she is fettered to the land and to a low social class, thus, by and large, out of step with an urban, cosmopolitan, and neoliberal subject position, understood as significant components in the globalization of Swedish culture at the turn of the twenty-first century.[34] In fact, we see an anonymization of the regional Swedish space, a portrayal that seems to indicate that the uniform three-story housing tracts featured in many of these productions could be anywhere in dilapidated Europe.

Landscapes in many films coproduced by regional production centers resolutely turn away from any beautification of landscape and from recognizably localizing it. A small town may be featured in the filming location (most of these films make limited use of studio space), but it appears generic and anonymous. That is the case in Lars von Trier's *Dancer in the Dark* (2000), set in Washington State but shot exclusively in the environs of Trollhättan and coproduced by Film i Väst. In this film, the Swedish landscape is easily recognizable and spatial confusion offers some comical effects. As Björk sings her way along the Göta Älv with freighters bound for Göteborg in the background, she is accompanied by the sound of indigenous blackbirds. *Dancer in the Dark* is a significant example of how a Swedish landscape appears so anonymous and malleable that it can almost stand in for a very different location. Björk's character is notably going blind—she cannot see the particularities of the local landscape around her, and spectators seem invited to disregard its particularities, too.[35] The star power associated with this and other von Trier films shot at Trollhättan seem to make up for the fact that the films refuse any geographical or production-location specificity.[36]

Though a film like *Show Me Love* effectively deconstructs what has been touted in national film history as the distinctive beauty of the Swedish landscape, Moodysson's film is one of many shot in Sweden around the millennium that drastically re-imagines cinematic location construction. As such, films like *Show Me Love* exemplify a global phenomenon from a different perspective as regards location substitutions, production outsourcing, and runaway productions. As Toby Miller and his coauthors emphasize in *Global Hollywood 2*, better-known examples include using Vancouver for Los Angeles or Toronto for New York.[37] More specifically, the term "de-localization" has been used to describe transitions in the European film industry since the early 1990s, as it has come to rely extensively on transnational coproduction[38] agreements that effectively partake in wide-ranging location substitution, as one country or location stands in for another.[39] *Show Me Love* can help us understand the significance of this geographical complexity.

Åmål in Trollywood: On Location and Film i Väst

Moodysson's *Show Me Love* offers insights into cultural connotations of location substitution on a local level. To return once more to the significant bridge-over-the-highway-to-Stockholm location, we should note that the sign "Welcome to Åmål" is clearly discernible in the background. The sign was manufactured specifically for the film. Indeed, Åmål's municipal government expressed great concern when they found out a film called *Fucking Åmål* was in production and initially wanted nothing to do with it.[40] They refused to let the film team use one of the town's own signs (though these are public property), and instead a new one was manufactured and installed in Trollhättan. This disagreement over the use of a sign—and Moodysson's insistence that *Show Me Love* should include in its mise-en-scène an artificial reference to a real town—indicates tensions embedded in cinematic location substitution. For an international viewer, the difference between Trollhättan and Åmål may seem negligible and irrelevant to the story; in fact, the depiction of the small town appeared "authentic" and "realistic" to most reviewers who commented on it. For the local inhabitants of Åmål and Trollhättan, though, the difference between the production location and the cinematic representation of location was not a matter of insignificant details. And neither was it for Moodysson, nor, I argue, for its Swedish audiences. The idea of local specificity embedded in *Show Me Love*'s plot and its production design became a vehicle not only for rethinking national cultural connotations of the film industry but also for questioning a perception that a particular location could—or should—grant authenticity to the cinematic product.

Åmål is a hamlet of about 12,000 inhabitants on the large lake Vänern in the province of Dalsland. It has served as a stereotypical image of the Swedish small town for many decades, including as the butt of jokes that thematize provincial insularity and close-mindedness.[41] One journalist describes Åmål as, in fact, "idyllic," though after viewing Moodysson's film he had expected it to be "depressingly gray," but its "old wooden buildings and river meandering through" remind him of an "illustrated children's book."[42] Conveying a sense for what teenage life would be like specifically in the small town of Åmål was a driving force for Moodysson. With members of the film team, he went to Åmål to observe the apparel, social practices, and language of the town's youth, and also conducted some ad hoc interviews. "I think they were wondering what we were doing in their town." Moodysson adds, "I am not quite sure myself why we did these things. But I knew I wanted the film to feel like it could be Åmål."[43] He also asked production designer Lina Strand and costume designer Maria Svensson to visit Åmål teenagers in their homes and make notes of how their houses, clothes, and personal items looked. "I think we could just as well have remained in Trollhättan," he continues, "but anything that had to do with Åmål felt like it was magic. It became like the holy grail."[44]

Moodysson's interest in authenticity extends to his representation of place. "I am very interested in space. Locations matter. I have a feeling that all places and environments carry traces of people who have been there. Places have a history that influences our perception of them in the present."[45] Moodysson maintains that his screenplay was heavily influenced by walks around the small town of Kungälv, about two hours south of Åmål, where he was living at the time of writing the *Show Me Love* script.[46] Walking the housing tracts that look just like the ones Elin inhabits, he tried imagining what life would have been like for young women there. In several ways, then, this specific script's origin conflates the specificity of location with the perceived anonymity of the three-story suburban apartment building. By extension, the anonymity of the small-town setting and the fact that it could be anywhere in Europe provided a plausible setting for *Show Me Love*.

Moodysson's work methods emphasize thorough attention to detail in the production design, as many who have worked with him attest.[47] These methods also testify to a sense of the practitioner's agency—namely, that cinematic representation is shaped by material aspects of the locale, like objects, props, and spaces. Moodysson's careful work demonstrates that these aspects matter to the production, whether they are recognizable to audiences or even deemed relevant by them. Moodysson's comments on his strategies and interests as a filmmaker make reference to questions of authenticity, of seeking to realistically portray a slice of life at a given moment in time. On the other hand, the supposedly genuine depiction of this small town is one that is entirely fabricated, down to the signpost "Welcome to Åmål." In hindsight, the team's reverie for the small town of Åmål appears ironically indicative of later discourses on globalization as it erases difference and disregards specificity in its supposed search for authenticity. The substitution of Trollhättan for Åmål may seem like a small detail, but it in fact helps illustrate conceptions of the local and regional. What *Show Me Love* supposedly contributes to Swedish film around the turn of the millennium is in fact part of an imaginary geographical vision that conflates two distinct places in the eyes of the public, most of which, like the non-locals on the film team and director Moodysson, have little or no personal experience in these small towns.

Trollhättan, in contrast to Åmål, is a working-class manufacturing town, an important site for heavy machinery and transportation industry since the mid-nineteenth century. In the 1940s it became a site of production for Saab automobiles. Dominated by the Social Democratic Party since the mid-1930s, Trollhättan was viewed in Sweden as a paragon of the kind of prosperity and stability produced by the Swedish welfare state since the end of the Second World War. But by the early 1990s it faced high unemployment and a shrinking tax base. It had become associated, as Allan Pred has shown, with an increasing Swedish intolerance toward an emerging multiethnic social complexity.[48] A 1993 Mosque burning and neo-Nazi-instigated violence, including the murder of a Somali refugee at the city's main square, created a media frenzy, and Swedes started "equating Trollhättan with racism."[49] The racial tension that came to the forefront in Trollhättan reflects Sweden's transition into a fully multiethnic society by the mid-1990s. Statistics vary, but a United Nations report claimed that in 1995, more than 10 percent of the Swedish population was born abroad, with first- or second-generation immigrants comprising nearly 20 percent.[50]

Characters and actors in *Show Me Love* are, however, ethnically homogenous. They are all white. The town and its inhabitants appear frozen in a time when modern Sweden was imagined as ethnically homogenous (though it of course never was so; larger-scale employment immigration began in the early 1960s, and it has always included a significant Sámi population in the north).[51] The real Åmål may have received a smaller allocation of asylum seekers and refugee immigrants than did Trollhättan in the early 1990s and might, for this reason, have been an intriguing imaginary location for Moodysson, a kind of zero degree location of cultural Swedishness. The absence of multiethnic representation thus makes the film appear completely "Swedish." But *Show Me Love* complicates any such notion and offers a window into the tensions embedded in European national film culture at the end of the twentieth century.

Though the de facto location substitution—Trollhättan for Åmål—challenges the authenticity claim Moodysson seeks to make about his film, *Show Me Love* is credited with helping turn around the image of Trollhättan. Moodysson and Tomas Eskilsson, founder and CEO of the regional production center Film i Väst, are thought of as principal players in revitalizing a popular perception of Trollhättan at the end of the 1990s. A parochial, provincial, and racist stigma was substituted by credible cosmopolitan pretensions, seemingly deserving of its moniker Trollywood. Trollhättan has been home to the regional film production center Film i Väst since 1997.[52] In the early 1990s, Eskilsson took the lead in formulating policy for developing a regional film industry in western Sweden. He worked closely with local municipalities and counties, as well as with Gunnar Carlsson of public service television SvT Göteborg, in efforts to establish the area around Trollhättan as a domestic *and* international center for film production.[53] Hardly any feature films had been shot in this region since the 1940s. Few insiders in the Swedish film industry took the initiative seriously at first. *Show Me Love* was the first feature film coproduced by Film i Väst to be released. Moodysson describes *Show Me Love* as participating in a big experiment, as the team was trying to figure out how to make a film in a location where there was, in fact, little film production infrastructure at the end of the 1990s. Moodysson has repeatedly emphasized in interviews the spirit of a pioneering film production he encountered in Trollhättan. He describes Trollhättan as "genuine"; working there was like "entering reality" rather than a "drama factory."[54] Moodysson expresses great satisfaction with having shot at least part of all his films there. "People in town really seem to enjoy the presence of a film team. When we shot the scene at the fast food joint [*korvkiosk*] in *Show Me Love*, we filmed right in the center of town, surrounded by spectators; we used the same *korvkiosk* in my subsequent film *Together*."[55] This kind of endorsement of the film industry and its warm reception in Trollhättan and neighboring cities such as Vänersborg has been effectively promoted by Film i Väst, including in its publication *Drömfabriken*, which appears in an abbreviated English version, *Film Factory*. It features numerous interviews with locals who have become involved in film production and with other residents.

Moodysson maintains that his approach to production design for *Show Me Love* stems from both the local production circumstances and his general understanding of his role as director. The team seems to have made a virtue of the nonexistent resources and found suitable on-location sites through local networks.[56] Shunning studio shots—with the exception of the school bathroom scene— *Show Me Love*'s production design effectively emphasizes the local and the specific. Moodysson says that he sought a non-hierarchical model of cooperation within all the functions of the team. "To give an example, I relied on and trusted Kalle (Karl) Strandlind's sense of place," Moodysson explains, "though he was young and not very high up in the hierarchy of a traditional film shoot, but he played a critical role in finding the right locations for *Show Me Love*. And for a person like Kalle, a local without previous interest in film production, the non-hierarchical co-operative model of *Show Me Love* worked well. I don't think he has continued working in film production with other directors since." *Show Me Love* location manager Anna Malini Ahlberg hired the young local handyman Strandlind as location researcher, and he drove her and Moodysson around to scout for locations—the school, Elin's apartment, and Agnes' house. Moodysson's and the team's interest in the local and the specific indicates how the regionalization of the Swedish film industry not only changed production parameters, but also put the small town and its inhabitants on the Swedish map of popular culture. Moodysson's collaborative methods for his first film in Trollhättan also illustrate other aspects of a transition in film production, namely its transition from a historically auteur-based and nationally centralized to collective and decentralized.[57]

The geography of *Show Me Love* is thus more complex than may be assumed at first. In fact, the production, funding, and filming locations of *Show Me Love* help illustrate fundamental shifts in the Swedish and European film industries since the mid-1990s. The shifts, especially in terms of funding and filming location, further position *Show Me Love* as a significant cultural artifact of its time both in Sweden and internationally. The regional production center Film i Väst became a way of making outsider films for Moodysson and many of other Swedish directors in the late 1990s. These films challenged the cultural elite in Stockholm and, by implication, conceptions of film made in Sweden along national lines. *Show Me Love* in many ways contributed to a popular understanding of the regionalization of the Swedish film industry in the late 1990s. *Show Me Love* also contributed to making the regionalization efforts of the European Union visible in contemporary Swedish popular culture. The film seemed to emphasize the small-town locality as a source of authenticity, while in fact *Show Me Love*'s production was part and parcel of much larger transitions in the Swedish film industry that extend far beyond any small Swedish town.

Show Me Love, Film i Väst, and a Cultural Understanding of European Union Regionalization

What can the interplay between the imaginary space of an anonymous small Swedish town and a burgeoning film industry in another small town tell us about Sweden and Europe? Part of what makes

Show Me Love such a significant cultural artifact is that it became one of the first films to indicate how Sweden's entry into the European Union could be reflected in popular culture. The film shows an increasing regionalization of the Swedish economy after Sweden's entry into the European Union in 1995.

EU regionalization initiatives can be understood as operating along two distinct but complementary lines. First, the EU emphasizes the creation of regional economic structures on a subnational level, exemplified by the establishment of the large county of Västra Götaland as a new administrative entity in 1998 (Göteborg is the largest city in this county and Trollhättan is one of its many smaller municipalities). Second, the EU fosters the creation of transnational economic regions, which operate across national borders (the Oresund region, bridging southernmost Sweden and the Copenhagen area of Denmark, is one example). Regional policy measures comprise about 30 percent of the EU budget. In this way, the EU calls simultaneously for (supranational) integration *and* (subnational) regionalization. As Michael Keating has shown, "There is, at first glance, a contradiction between the two trends, since European integration takes matters to a supranational level, while regionalism is concerned with strengthening the subnational level. Yet there are also elements of consistency and mutual reinforcement in the two movements."[58] One of the most significant of these elements is that regionalization seeks to delimit the power and significance of the nation-state. This element is significant when it comes to film production, since European cinema has been understood and marketed as a national product for many years.

The European Commission and other EU agencies emphasize film production as part of the "central role of culture in the process of European integration."[59] The regionalization of the film industry in Sweden illustrates this policy mandate. Funding from the EU's

European Regional Development Fund (ERDF) for economically depressed regions made Film i Väst into a significant film production center. Under the leadership of CEO Tomas Eskilsson and with broad local support from Trollhättan and surrounding municipalities in the county of Västra Götaland, Film i Väst applied for and received European Union structural funds for economic revitalization. Funds were awarded in 1997 with the purpose of stimulating the local economy; during its first years of funding, Film i Väst channeled EU funds slated for regional economic development into film production.[60] *Show Me Love* is a cultural artifact that allows us to understand the regionalization and denationalization of the Swedish film industry following EU membership. Film i Väst provided about a third of the film's budget, and the end credits specify that the film was produced with the help of EU funds. Moodysson's perception is that Film i Väst gave him critical and necessary support: "They were interested in coproducing the film right away," while the Swedish Film Institute initially declined awarding the project funding.[61] This film may appear Swedish, but its funding structure helps illustrate how it can be seen as the first cultural artifact to make the European Union visible in Swedish popular culture.

The success of Film i Väst has been particularly significant for the regionalization of the Swedish film industry (there are a number of similar regional production centers in Sweden, but Film i Väst is the largest). Though Sweden's entry into the EU sped up the regionalization of the film industry on the subnational level, Film i Väst was able to build on a regional film policy that had been in place in Sweden since the early 1980s. This policy mandated that the entire Swedish population should have access to quality film.[62] A wider implication of the film policy is that metropolitan areas (i.e., Stockholm) cannot be the only locations featured in films paid for with taxpayer funds.

This initiative complements publicly funded regional theaters and museums that help counteract the centralization of Swedish cultural production primarily in Stockholm and its environs. By the mid-1990s there was a gradual recognition that film production should no longer be conceived primarily in terms of a *national* art form. There was a movement away from regulating cinema through national culture politics in the form of state subventions for film institutes based in the capitals (kulturpolitik) and a movement toward *regional* economic revitalization by and through the film industry.[63] Sweden's entry into the European Union in 1995 provided the practical means to implement this vision.

Film i Väst has experienced astonishing growth. It is among the largest film production centers in Europe.[64] In 1998, the year of *Show Me Love*'s release, Film i Väst coproduced eight films. In 2002, the year of Moodysson's *Lilya 4-ever*, Film i Väst coproduced thirteen films. By the mid-2000s, Film i Väst was coproducing between fifteen and twenty films per year, with about a dozen of those in production and the remainder as part of postproduction support. By 2009 the yearly number had risen to 21. By 2010 Film i Väst had coproduced nearly 250 feature films, as well as numerous documentaries, short films, and drama productions for television.[65] Many of the films coproduced by Film i Väst have won national and international awards at A-list festivals such as Cannes and Berlin. The spatial and cultural implications of the regionalization of the Swedish film industry had a significant impact on Moodysson as a director and help us understand how an EU membership also translates into cultural representation.

From 1997 to 2000 EU funds awarded to Film i Väst were channeled directly into production. During the period 2002–2005 EU funding could no longer be channeled into production support and instead went to infrastructure investments, such as the construction of studios and postproduction facilities. Film i Väst funding has come primarily from the county of Västra Götaland and local municipalities since 2005; initially Film i Väst also received funding from the Swedish Film Institute. Film i Väst has grown substantially since Moodysson made *Show Me Love*, with revenue increasing threefold between 1998 and 2009 and annual awarded production support reaching over SEK 70 million in recent years.[66] Film i Väst functions as a coproducer, film commission, and regional resource center. Its permanent studio is the second largest in Scandinavia and the center provides access to quality postproduction facilities, serves as a network hub for local film service companies, and facilitates access to film industry craftspeople. The local university college, Högskolan i Väst, has developed a film worker technical training program for industry professionals in the region.

Most regional film centers in Sweden and Europe have different funding requirements, but a majority requires local spending and the use of the local infrastructure and personnel. Three of Moodysson's feature films, *Show Me Love*, *Together*, and *A Hole in My Heart*, were shot exclusively in Trollhättan; his other films combine location and studio shooting in Trollhättan with other filming in international locations, as in *Lilya 4-ever*, *Container*, and *Mammoth*. Film i Väst has required localized film production in the region as a condition for coproduction funding, and Moodysson's films have been among the most highly profiled by the center and Swedish media. In 1998 Film i Väst could finance up to one-third of a feature film deemed to be of high artistic merit and with audience potential. That percentage has since decreased. The agency also requires that any coproduction funding contribute to strengthening the region's film production infrastructure. At the end of the 1990s Film i Väst required in return that at least 50 percent of all people involved in the production have their domicile within the Västra Götaland county, that production take place in at least one of four local municipalities in the Trollhättan region, and that at least a sum equivalent to the funding be spent exclusively in the region. It was also expected that the main producer would have an office with personnel in Trollhättan. The regional production center continues to straddle a mission of seeking to create economic improvement, employment opportunities, and representing the region as a desirable location to live and work, with an emphasis on coproducing quality films, expanding international coproductions, and fostering emerging directors.

Film i Väst has combined different kinds of public funding (EU, national, regional, and municipal) to emulate a business enterprise in a cultural sector of the economy where there was no historical basis for this kind of economic engagement. The net economic impact of Film i Väst has been disputed by scholars, however. Per Assmo and others have argued that it is not clear that film production has had measurable economic effects in the region. Seen from this perspective, Film i Väst is a paper product that would collapse if the county of Västra Götaland did not pour tax-funded support into it. In this sense it is a *biståndsprojekt* (foreign aid project) for a deindustrializing Sweden. But Film i Väst continues to coproduce films and has effectively transformed the Swedish film industry by simultaneously regionalizing *and* internationalizing it.

Though Film i Väst may at first appear to be a regional entity that attracts predominantly Swedish filmmakers to make films in Swedish for a primarily Swedish audience, part of its enduring impact stems from the fact that it has effectively helped internationalize the Swedish film industry. By the mid-2000s Film i Väst presented itself in marketing material as "the foremost film production region in northern Europe [with] films produced [that] are of high quality and competitive on the international market."[67] The international component of Film i Väst was part of its initial pitch to the Västra Götaland county and local municipalities for support. Eskilsson invited Lars Jönsson, producer of Memfis Film, and Peter Aalbaek Jensen, producer and founder of Zentropa Productions, to Trollhättan in the mid-1990s to present to them his idea for a film production center there. Jönsson and Aalbaek Jensen were initially skeptical, but a majority of Jönsson's films on the Memfis label (including those directed by Moodysson) and a number of Zentropa films (including many by Lars von Trier) have subsequently been coproduced and at least partially shot in Trollhättan.[68]

The development of regional film production centers was not a phenomenon confined to Sweden in the 1990s. Film production centers had been developed in Sheffield and Düsseldorf in the 1980s with the explicit mandate of counteracting negative economic effects of deindustrialization.[69] In the early 1990s a number of regions in Europe began planning for locally supported regional film production. By 2004 there were 79 regions in Europe with significant film production initiatives.[70] Recent European film scholarship, however, has tended to overlook the critical significance of regional film production centers.[71] This is despite the fact that regional film centers have transformed film production in Europe since the early 1990s. The impact of these centers continues to be significant. In fact, for many filmmakers, regional funding has provided critical resources. In 2008 about 20 percent of all funding for feature film production in Europe came from regional centers.[72] EU funding slated for regional economic development, awarded to Film i Väst and subsequently channeled directly into film production, illustrates how popular culture can help us understand tensions among the regional, national, and supranational that are part of contemporary Europe.

Show Me Love and Regional, National, and Transnational European Film Production

Show Me Love's spatial anonymity—its generic apartment buildings, its highway overpass, its middle-class interiors—offers a pragmatic example for understanding a turn from film as national product to one that is simultaneously regional and, as part of European Union promoted efforts, also supranational. The film's funding and conditions of production illustrate how these changes are "influenced from above in the shape of globalization and of European integration,"[73] though Moodysson's interest in Åmål and Trollhättan reflects that these changes originate also "from below in the shape of regional and local initiatives."[74] Yet paradigms of the national in both European cinema production and film historiography remain strong. Jill Forbes and Sarah Street argue that "European governments were led to attempt to define a national film since this was both a form of distinctiveness and a useful counterweight to the supposed 'universalism' of Hollywood."[75] Scholars point to the close association between European auteur and art films made in the director's native language and subsequently exported outside the country of origin as distinctive for that particular nation.

The prominence of European coproductions in the 1950s and 1960s shows, however, that the "idea of 'pure' national film cultures is a myth."[76] The "concept of national cinema [is] a regulative idea, a vision in tension . . . with the transnational realities of cinematic production that have characterized filmmaking for many decades," Mette Hjort argues.[77] Yet, the effects of this mythic national coding (Galt) or regulative idea (Hjort) have remained strong. Thomas Elsaesser argues that for decades Ingmar Bergman's films "defined both to his countrymen and to the rest of the world what 'Swedish' (cinema) meant."[78] This view is echoed by Eva af Geijerstam's description of Ingmar Bergman as "an ambassador of Swedish culture."[79] But Bergman made films explicitly for an international audience and sometimes through transnational production paradigms. His German-American coproduction *The Serpent's Egg* (*Ormens ägg*, 1977) constitutes one aspect of the Swedish director's transnational production, as it was made at Bavaria Film Studios in West Germany with actors and funding sources from multiple national origins. Moodysson's later films (especially *Mammoth*) actually follow a similar pattern. Nevertheless, Elsaesser's reference to the national components of Swedish cinema is apt. The film industry in Sweden had stronger national importance; there were more state-mandated policies regarding film; and cinema culture itself was more popular—all of which contrasts with many other European countries.

A centralized and nationally conceived film culture dominated in Sweden longer than in other European countries. Though there were some international coproductions made in Sweden that received funding from the Swedish Film Institute during the 1960s, 1970s, and 1980s,[80] Swedish film production during these decades was largely a national affair, centralized in Stockholm.[81] In the first half of the century an increasing number of depictions of the small town and provincial countryside in the 1930s was at least partly a result of the proliferation of small production companies located also outside of Stockholm. Since the early 1960s, however, "film production was centralized in Stockholm, which limited the number of and impact from films that thematized provincial life."[82] Through the end of the 1980s, "Film policy in Sweden was wholly a [Stockholm-centered] national affair."[83] Stockholm was the central location for film companies with large studios in the capital region, such as Svensk filmindustri, Sandrew, and Europa Film, and institutions like Dramatiska

Institutet, Filmhuset, and multiple theaters (for example, The Royal Dramatic Theatre) with high-profile actors who often crossed over into film and their performance industry personnel. The emphasis on Swedish film as a national cultural product through the late 1980s also stems from the continued significance of the Swedish Film Institute. The state-authorized Film Production and Distribution Treaty of 1963 (*filmavtalet*) enabled SFI to award substantial production funds to Swedish filmmakers, provide film production venues in its studios and postproduction facilities in Stockholm, and facilitate the marketing of films made in Sweden as "Swedish."[84]

At the end of the 1980s cultural attitudes and policy had changed in Europe regarding film production. Policy, production, and distribution began to be regionalized but in two different and somewhat contradictory ways. One aspect of this regionalization process emphasized the region as a subnational area targeted for economic development; another aspect involved the transnational conception of a Nordic region as reflected through film production. Both aspects of this regionalization were significant for Moodysson and *Show Me Love*. The Nordic region comprises the five countries Denmark, Finland, Iceland, Norway, and Sweden (and their related territories) and has been officially organized as the intergovernmental forum the Nordic Council since 1952. This council was implemented largely as a response to the Cold War, as a perceived counterbalance to the Nordic region's precarious geopolitical location between two superpowers. It is best known in the public imagination as the agency that implemented passport-free travel among the Nordic countries as early as the mid-1950s. Today it is known for its promotion of environmental and cultural issues, especially the high-profile Nordic Council literary prize awarded annually.

The Nordic Council established the Nordic Film and Television

Fund (NFTF) in 1990. With the NFTF, film production in northernmost Europe rapidly became transnational. The purpose of the fund is to "promote the production and distribution of audiovisual projects in Nordic countries."[85] In order to receive funding, "A film has to be guaranteed theatrical distribution in a minimum of two Nordic countries and have a broadcast agreement with at least one of the fund's TV partners," while there are no requirements on pan-Nordic themes or national quotas.[86] Coproduction funding could originally be sought from the NFTF if there were more than two Nordic countries involved in a film's A-list functions, such as director, producer, leading actors, and so on (after 1994 this production clause was done away with). NFTF funding has had a dynamic impact on film production in the region, with new collaborations inaugurated across national borders. Many films have been exported, distributed, and marketed within the individual countries of the Nordic region.[87] *Show Me Love* did not receive NFTF support, but it did receive funding from both the Danish and Swedish Film Institutes, and the Danish Zentropa coproduced the film with Memfis, the main production company.

One effect of the change to a transnational regional film culture in the 1990s was that Nordic cinema went from largely monolingual, as reflective of an earlier emphasis on film as a national cultural product, to sometimes confusingly multilingual. Jan Troell's film *Hamsun* (1996) is an intriguing example, as Trevor Elkington and Andrew Nestingen argue. A Swedish actor plays the Norwegian author and a Danish actor plays his equally Norwegian wife. The film is directed by a Swede (Troell); shot in Norway; produced by a Danish company (Nordisk Film A/S) with funding sources from Denmark, Norway, Sweden, and Germany; supported by the NFTF and Eurimages; and operates in three distinct national languages—Swedish, Norwegian, and Danish.[88] As Elkington and Nestingen make clear, "*Hamsun*'s relative international success despite ignorance [outside of the Nordic region] of its historical and national particularities indicates just how little nation matters as a category in what is ostensibly a national prestige film."[89]

Approved and implemented at around the same time as the NFTF, the 1992 European Convention on Cinematographic Coproduction had a significant impact on film production in the Nordic region and specifically Sweden. The convention facilitates coproductions across national borders and essentially provides a model and vehicle for the widespread coproduction funding mechanisms available in Europe today. Other significant European funding programs include the MEDIA programs sponsored by the European Union, which grant funding primarily for pre- and postproduction, and the European Council program Eurimages, which grants funding primarily for distribution. These programs have turned European film production from a nation-based industry to an international and transnational one. *Show Me Love* may in fact seem distinctly Swedish, especially to an international audience (and international reviews support such a reading)—the director and all A-list roles are Swedish, the main production company, Memfis, is Swedish, and the cast and characters all speak Swedish and are all ethnically homogenous and white. Still this film is part of a new transnational context.

Show Me Love, International Funding Sources, and the Production Company Memfis

Though funding from the Swedish Film Institute and coproduction funds from the regional film production center Film i Väst have been significant for Moodysson's career, his involvement with the production company Memfis offers a complementary perspective on the changing geography of the Swedish film industry in the 1990s. Memfis, in fact, exercised one of the strongest influences on the Swedish film industry from the mid-1990s until around 2005. As Mikael Timm argues, the 1990s can be seen as the decade of the producer.[90] Moodysson's trajectory as a filmmaker has been shaped by his close association with Memfis and has benefited from Memfis' stable transnational funding paradigm, which includes Swedish Film Institute funds, regional film center coproduction funds (usually from Film i Väst), Swedish Television (SvT) funds, coproduction funds from Zentropa (which allows it to request funding from the Danish Film Institute), the NFTF, and its own production company funds. The funding sources of *Show Me Love* effectively underscore the transitions in the Swedish film industry at the end of the 1990s. Of a total budget of SEK 9 million (roughly 1 million USD), Film i Väst awarded approximately SEK 3 million, the Swedish Film Institute SEK 2.5 million, and the Danish film institute SEK 1.15. Memfis and Zentropa provided the rest. Though unusual, Memfis has invested its own capital in the majority of its films, which, as Jönsson states, has significance on a number of levels. "Providing a chunk of the financing ourselves," Jönsson states, "gives us credibility and a clear stake in the process and allows us to keep full control over any given project. Of the twenty-five Memfis films produced by 2009, ten have given such significant profit that it has allowed us to reinvest in other films."[91]

Memfis Film has played a significant role in the Swedish film community and for the Swedish film industry since its inception in 1989. Several of its films, including Moodysson's, make up the core of a particularly strong group of Swedish films from 1998 to 2004.[92] Memfis is also one of the film companies that has consistently contributed to the decentralization of Swedish film production, though its office is located in Stockholm. Memfis' first major successful collaboration was with UK-born director Colin Nutley in the film *House of Angels* (*Änglagård*, 1992), which provided a prototype for many of Memfis' most successful later productions with regard to funding and location shooting—including Moodysson's *Show Me Love*. *House of Angels* was a blockbuster in Sweden and was screened all over the world, including distribution by Sony Classics in the United States. The film is set in a small rural village in the province of Västergötland (what is today part of the Västra Götaland region), far from the social and cultural context of contemporary Stockholm.[93] *Show Me Love* continued that approach a few years later. *House of Angel*'s formidable success provided Memfis with economic and cultural capital to channel into other projects and to attract quality talent. The success of *House of Angels* also helped institute Jönsson's long-term collaborative relationship with Peter Aalbaek Jensen and Lars von Trier, founders of what has become contemporary Scandinavia's most important production company—Zentropa. Together, these producers established a successful coproduction model that combined transnational, national, and regional funding, including television funding for cinema productions.[94] The combination of funding resources became such a stable model for Memfis that it gave the company freedom to pursue unknown and emerging directors and to some extent unconventional film topics—including in particular those of Moodysson's later films.[95] It has also allowed for concrete and hands-on involvement in all stages of the film production process, including close collaborations with directors who write their own screenplays. Memfis also had a significant importance for the reach of Swedish and Scandinavian film outside the Nordic region. International distribution of films from small countries and narrow language areas is complicated, yet one of the ways in which a film can become part of the canon within national and international contexts derives from its exposure outside the nation in which it was conceived. But for this to occur there must be reliable channels of distribution. Trust Film Sales, one of the most important international distributors of Swedish and Danish films during the last decade, was jointly founded by Jönsson/Memfis and Aalbaek Jensen/Zentropa in the mid-1990s.[96] *Show Me Love* was one of the first films distributed internationally by Trust Films.

Memfis' significance for Swedish film both domestically and internationally was recently made manifest in the collection of twenty-three DVDs released in 2009, of which Moodysson's features make up one-fifth of the collection. These Memfis films represent a significant component of modern Swedish film history, and this DVD set is remarkable for several reasons. First, it makes concrete and visible Memfis' contribution not only to Swedish but to contemporary world cinema. A set like this assumes the status of a collector's item and suggests that the films produced by this production company will remain a part of the cinematic canon for a significant period of time. All the films offer English subtitles (most are also subtitled in other Nordic languages), which indicates that Memfis is aware that its contribution to film history extends beyond the borders of Sweden. Assembled as a collection, this set also suggests that Memfis films form a cohesive whole and have their own iconicity; this seems modeled on the practice of re-releasing the films of major directors and auteurs as DVD collections. In fact, few contemporary Swedish production companies could have re-released twenty-three films. With the exception of the traditional behemoths Svensk filmindustri (founded in 1919) and its competitor Sandrews (founded in the 1920s), Memfis is one of few quality film production companies that remained in business and capable of producing a steady stream of films meriting re-release. Lastly, the DVD set indicates Memfis' savvy marketing and positioning strategies—one of its strengths has been its close attention to the packaging and marketing of its films, including those of Moodysson.

I have addressed some of the ways in which transformations in the European and Scandinavian film industry over the last decade or so can be understood through representations of cinematic landscapes. A film like *Show Me Love* illustrates how regional coproduction centers like Film i Väst are now an integral part of how films are funded, made, and shot. These centers also determine in part which images of particular locations get distributed around the world. *Show Me Love*'s landscape and location in fact replicate the tensions and challenges thematically addressed in the film, which are also embedded in the parameters of production and filming. Though the setting of the rural countryside has historically lent itself to comedic representations of country bumpkins, literary adaptations, heritage and costume dramas, or romantic comedies that pit the city outsider against the rural collective, *Show Me Love*, within its aesthetic form and production history, draws attention to the location in which it is set and shot, a unique choice of setting that also secured part of the production funding. The film takes the small-town and regional context and turns it into a primary location to challenge heteronormativity and conventional representations of high school, and it offers landscapes that are far from prettified. The film's refusal of aesthetic escapism is significant because it provides a different perspective on the mandate for regional economic development that underlies some of the coproduction funding. A center like Film i Väst is concerned with fostering employment and increasing economic activity, and *Show Me Love* does not embellish the landscape as to somehow gloss over the region's socioeconomic reality. *Show Me Love* also presents a different image of contemporary Sweden to audiences both domestic and international. It breaks with conventional understandings of "Swedishness"—including the traditional depiction of Swedish landscapes and natural beauty. It also locates the small town at the center of globalization, EU policy implementation, and the whitewashing of racial and ethnic tensions in contemporary Swedish culture.

Regional production centers are not, of course, unique to Sweden—the UK, Ireland, Germany, France, Romania, and Poland, among others, all have such centers. The fact that a film is shot in a certain regional center may be completely irrelevant to most viewers, and a film in Swedish with a Swedish director and a largely Swedish cast would appear to most viewers to be "Swedish" rather than a regional production featuring Västra Götaland. Just as regional funding offers an incentive for film producers, the regional centers must market themselves both to the film industry and to their own regional constituencies that in most cases supply the public funding for the centers. Depictions of local landscapes are therefore not merely abstract, aesthetic features of a production: the filmic representation of a certain region can have real economic consequences depending on the attractiveness of a particular region. Films made at regional centers also depend on the free movement of people, employment, and services within Europe, so that, for example, a UK director can make a film with his hand-picked A-list functions in Sweden which subsequently will be sold to virtually all EU countries. Such a production would showcase a particular form of Swedish landscape to those viewers, as has been the case recently with the BBC-initiated adaptations of Henning Mankell's works shot in English with Kenneth Branagh in the title role on location in Skåne in southern Sweden.[97] Regional films and their representations of landscapes come to express the tenets of European Union rhetoric and policy in popular culture, albeit in different and often oblique ways; labeling European films according to national labels actually masks the fact that the regional production centers encourage the de-emphasis on the nation-state promoted by the European Union in favor of cultivating regional identity.

4

Moodysson's Continuation

Lukas Moodysson's trajectory as a script writer and director after *Show Me Love* demonstrates a continued interest in contemporary social observation, representations of gender and sexual practices, and in crafting compelling young characters, whose clear-sighted perspectives reveal the conceits of the adult world and the political establishment. Whereas *Show Me Love* investigates the insularity and confinement of small-town life, later projects expand the range of inquiry to the construction of both contemporary Swedish national identity and globalization processes of the early twenty-first century. Like *Show Me Love*, later films reflect Moodysson's self-professed dedication to cinematic authenticity in their dialogues, characterization, or mise-en-scène and production design. These films also reflect an increasing interest in experimenting with and exploring film as a collective and collaborative medium. This chapter presents some of these themes and strategies in Moodysson's later films from *Together* (*Tillsammans*, 2000) to *Mammoth* (*Mammut*, 2009).[1]

Together is an ensemble film with multiple story lines and multiple strong characters. It is set in a commune in Stockholm in 1975 and focuses on the political and sexual exploration of a seemingly radical group of leftists, who relinquish the comforts (and the presumed false consciousness) of the Swedish Social Democratic welfare state. Siblings Göran (Gustaf Hammarsten) and Elisabeth (Lisa Lindgren) are the principal storytelling vehicles, and Elisabeth's thirteen-year-old daughter Eva (Emma Samuelsson) and eight-year-old son Stefan (Sam Kessel) function as critical interpretive filters. As in *Show Me Love* and *Lilya 4-ever*, Moodysson draws on children's perspectives to convey social commentary and level criticism at the adult world. The commune's political affiliations range from the mildly conservative to revolutionary communist, and sexual identities include the conventionally heterosexual as well as gay and lesbian. Construed as a microcosm of tensions within 1970s socialist movements in Sweden, and under the apt title "Together," the commune is also a commentary on the Social Democratic welfare state, the hegemonic political system of Sweden by the mid-1970s, and the belief in family-like solidarity required to maintain it.

Together was almost as successful in Sweden as *Show Me Love* and expanded Moodysson's international recognition.[2] The film did well in both the US and UK markets.[3] It landed the third spot in *Entertainment Weekly*'s list of the best films in 2001 and was featured on multiple US critics' lists of best films that year.[4] Though *Together* can be seen as an entertaining feel-good film, it is also a social satire and a significant historiographic exercise that addresses Sweden's recent past. Reviews and audience reactions in Sweden make clear that the film was received as a historical account—if part parody—of 1970s Sweden. It helped fill a cultural void of information about this era both for a younger generation and for the generation that had experienced some of the political, social, and sexual movements the film explores.

Making the film involved extensive research, including in terms of production design and the portrayal of domestic life on a commune. In *Together,* the commune's ten-room house is consequently more than a set. Moodysson wanted the collective's home to be a total immersion experience. In it, all objects were to be authentic and functional even to the level that actors could cook in the kitchen and sleep in the beds. There was a potato patch outside, a compost heap, laundry on clotheslines, and trash in the corners. "Every object was minutely selected and situated; there was not a corner in this ten-room house that was 'outside' the illusion," chief production designer Carl Johan de Geer emphasizes. The production design is part of what makes this film a significant cinematic and historiographic document. The scenography invites complete and full immersion in a domestic space—by both actors and audience.[5] In a commentary about his experience working with, and against, Moodysson's "iron will," de Geer extrapolates on the production design experiment in *Together*: "The actors felt at home in the house, as if it were their rooms, their books, their unmade beds." He continues, "I learned something; for the first time, I had seen how the production design could be a part of a director's method; that it could be meaningful for actors to have a complete environment constructed also when it may not be seen in the film."[6] The conceit of complete immersion helps illustrate the film's historiographic premise. It focuses on the (Swedish) home, the family, and the materiality of locations and objects as ways to comment on a historical moment known for political involvement across classes and world regions, including Sweden's official and nonofficial support for solidarity movements in the developing world.

The close association between the Swedish welfare state—fully instituted by the mid-1970s—and its historic association with the metaphor of home and domesticity has been amply discussed by a number of scholars and historians.[7] Tenets of the Social Democratic welfare state (including its rhetoric of egalitarianism, solidarity, and gender equality) inform *Together* on a number of levels. Centering the plot of the film in the domestic space of the collective *Together* brings up the Swedish Social Democratic concept of *folkhemmet* (the People's Home), a term coined by Social Democratic Party leader Per Albin Hansson in 1928. This term implies that the state, like a family, cares for its citizens from cradle to grave and fosters the analogy of the state as a household, to which all citizens, like family members, have a duty to contribute equally.[8] The film's collective represents a heterogeneous number of political views that, in fact, show the range of political positions lumped under the umbrella of socialism or social democracy. Yet the film pushes a middle-ground agenda of collectivism and community. This emphasis reflects Sweden's official policy during the Cold War, and especially during the 1970s, of seeking to forge a "third" or "middle" way, a centrist and neutral path in between two military superpowers that advocated radically different economic and social systems. Cold War tension is also reflected in *Together*'s characterization. Those not part of a middle-ground political collectivism are excluded in the final scene, in which a winter pickup game of soccer (the scene is dominated by pacifism's color white) celebrates group participation at the expense of (free market) competition or (rigorously planned) socialism.

In the early 2000s Moodysson's public statements about his films tend to emphasize social, emotional, and spiritual interests. He states that he wants his films to make a difference and that he wants to reach out and touch audiences. He sees his role as a filmmaker as one of providing guidance and hope.[9] "I really like people who try, people who dream, people who want to change things," Moodysson says. "I think we are living in a very, very political world . . . [where there are] enormous injustices. . . . I can maybe regret a little bit that I didn't make *Together* radical enough, politically speaking."[10] These statements are reflected in the script for the television miniseries *The New Country*, in *Lilya 4-ever* about trafficking and youth prostitution (by now an international classic), and in the lesser-known co-directed documentary *The Kids They Sentenced*.[11]

The New Country is a road movie whose script includes a clearly defined narrative arc and complex characters.[12] Two refugees and asylum seekers facing deportation (Somali-born teenager Ali, played by Mike Almayehu, and Iranian middle-aged man Massoud, played by Michalis Koutsogiannakis) are on the run from the Swedish authorities. Together with a former Miss Sweden pageant contestant and centerfold model (Louise, played by Lia Boysen), they try to escape from abuse and exploitation. The trio traverses a Swedish summer landscape and encounters an eclectic and often unsympathetic array of ethnic Swedes. Directed by Geir Hansteen Jörgensen, *The New Country* was broadcast on Swedish television in the spring of 2000; its final one-hour episode drew 1,450,000 viewers.[13] Critics have called it the best Swedish television miniseries ever.[14] *The New Country* reflects that by the year 2000 Swedish popular culture could no longer disregard the fact that the country had become multiethnic thanks to high immigration through the early 1990s. Since 1995, Sweden had been a member of the European Union, and its government and social policy were moving closer to neoliberal and globalization paradigms. In contrast to Moodysson's previous films, *The New Country* quickly became associated with a new wave of Swedish cinema that engaged multiculturalism and multiethnicity and helped fuel media discussions of "immigrant film" at the time.[15]

The Kids They Sentenced is a politically charged documentary that reflects Moodysson's and Stefan Jarl's indignation and incredulity about the Swedish establishment's reaction to public demonstrations against a European Union summit and visit by US president George W. Bush in Göteborg in June of 2001.[16] *The Kids They Sentenced* builds primarily on a dozen interviews with men and women sentenced for their participation in rallies or for having been involved in some organization. These are complemented by interviews with their parents. The film includes police and newsreel footage, as well as some recited poetry that thematizes the value of human and political solidarity. Some of the newsreel footage comes in the form of a montage that juxtaposes images of starving children (presumably in Africa), violent conflicts in the Middle East (Palestine, Iraq), warheads being deployed from ships at sea, medical animal experiments, and public demonstrations and rallies. This montage and the questioning technique gave rise to significant criticism in the Swedish media and the political establishment, which generally denounced the film as affectively overcharged and politically biased.[17] Distributed by the nonprofit small distributor Folkets Bio, the documentary had a limited run in theaters, but, given these limitations, it has attracted relatively large audiences.[18] Ultimately, the film's internal construction signals ambiguity: Is it a medium that gives "authentic voices" room for expression or is it a media montage in a modernist-avant-gardist tradition? In this sense, *The Kids They Sentenced* is consistent with the political and aesthetic ambiguity expressed by a number of Moodysson's films—*Show Me Love*, *Together*, and *Lilya 4-ever* included.

Like Moodysson's previous feature films, *Lilya 4-ever* garnered a great deal of media and critical attention, in Sweden as well as internationally. Although it reflects real events, this film is the fictional account of a young woman, Lilya (Oksana Akinshina), trafficked to Sweden for prostitution from an unnamed part of the former Soviet

Union.[19] *Lilya 4-ever* has been framed as Moodysson's most explicitly political film.[20] It is also his most openly religious film, seemingly inspired by divine intervention: "The story of the film came very suddenly to me. It was as if someone had whispered in my ear and said 'This is the film that you are going to make and you cannot do anything else.'"[21] In a number of paratexts surrounding *Lilya 4-ever*, including director's notes to the Swedish DVD version, Moodysson calls it a film about "God's benevolence" and says it aims to convey "hope" to the world. In an interview, Moodysson notes that it was originally "a more religious film." "It dealt with Jesus walking around in the world next to Lilya. He was physically one of the characters in the film."[22]

Lilya 4-ever is a conventional melodrama built on a rigid opposition between a young woman victimized by patriarchal social factors and geopolitical circumstances beyond her control. But the film also involves an attempt to recuperate religious humanism in contemporary secular and neoliberal Europe, a pattern congruent with Moodysson's characteristic ambivalence toward social issues. This marks *Lilya 4-ever* both as a moralizing spectacle *and* as an intriguing postmodernist religious exercise. The film reflects on real geopolitical circumstances, including human trafficking, transnational migration, and immigration. It thus addresses a renewed problematization of ethnic and religious identity in northern Europe during the last decades. At the same time, *Lilya 4-ever* (like a majority of Moodysson's films) draws on cinematic strategies and production choices that span a range of techniques and genre references. This highlights that the film's political and ethical messages are murkier than they initially appear.

Lilya 4-ever was lauded by Swedish politicians and journalists as an authentic and realistic portrayal of prostitution and trafficking.[23]

Critics generally disregarded the religious connotations of the film and focused instead on its political implications and gender themes. The film's release in August 2002 coincided with the implementation of a controversial new anti-prostitution law in Sweden that summer, which criminalized the purchase of sex rather than the selling of it.[24] *Lilya 4-ever* was subsequently used in government-authorized education initiatives both in Sweden and abroad.[25] The film won four *Guldbagge* awards in Sweden.[26] *Lilya 4-ever* was distributed internationally by the prestigious Newmarket Films, which attests to Moodysson's status as an acclaimed and internationally popular filmmaker at the time. International reviewers were largely positive toward the film, though many remarked on its dark tone and difficult subject matter and contrasted it with *Together* as a comedy.[27]

Lilya 4-ever simultaneously appears as an *exemplum* and as a modern allegory. At the same time it is curiously naive. Moodysson, like Lars von Trier in *Breaking the Waves*, appears to be referring to Catholicism's preoccupation with the tragic as is commonly understood in popular culture. In these films the world is in a fallen state and can only be partly redeemed by the sacrifice of an innocently pure child or young woman.[28] *Lilya 4-ever* links a political anti-trafficking and anti-prostitution agenda to an explicitly Christian framework. It even includes literal figurations of Lilya and Volodya (Artyom Bogucharsky) as angels on screen. Lilya's redemption, however, comes only through death; in life she is coded as a victim of her own mother's betrayal as well as of the betrayals of her mother country and of Sweden.[29] The figuration of Lilya as a victim operates on multiple levels—she is (ab)used in this film as a didactic vehicle that delivers a political message. She is also, arguably, part of a postmodernist experiment that reinserts a vaguely redemptive spirituality into a context marked by capitalist and political secularism.

On the other hand, the film reflects post-Soviet attitudes among youth toward religious practices during the 1990s. Lilya's own religiosity, her careful handling of an angel picture and repeated invocation of the Lord's Prayer, reflects Fran Markowitz's observations about Russian youth with regard to religion: It is, adolescents proclaim, an individualistic and personal choice, one that should not be publicly mandated or "publicly displayed."[30] Religious practice may be personal and individualistic for Lilya (indeed, no other character in the film partakes in any religious rituals), just as Moodysson describes it to be for himself, yet *Lilya 4-ever* materializes Christian iconography (Lilya and Volodya sprout wings). In so doing the film makes religious practice concrete, visible, and public. Moodysson's film, in fact, reflects on the "resurgence of religion that occurred throughout the former Soviet Union," which, Catherine Wanner and Mark Steinberg argue, "took many scholars and analysts by surprise, for they had come to think of socialist societies as thoroughly secular, if not atheist."[31]

For Moodysson, social commentary (in this film religious commentary) is always gendered and always formulated and expressed through sexual practices—in this case, Lilya's forced prostitution. This is part of what constitutes *Lilya 4-ever*'s ambivalence; it deals with gender and sexuality in connection with Christianity. If sexuality was a taboo topic in Soviet culture, as Markowitz outlines, it most certainly remains so in religious practices associated with the post-Soviet Orthodox Church.[32] Like many of Moodysson's films, *Lilya 4-ever* is fraught with ambivalent tensions. Lilya the victim also portrays individual spiritual redemption. *Lilya 4-ever*'s realistic portrayal of abuse and sexual violence is juxtaposed with a fantastical image of children-as-angels in death. The politically motivated reception of the film and its subsequent use in Swedish and international public information campaigns against trafficking and gender inequality contrast with Moodysson's idea about the film as a personal statement on God's benevolence.

After three internationally successful feature films (*Show Me Love*, *Together*, and *Lilya 4-ever*), Moodysson was courted by Hollywood producers in the early 2000s. Unlike some of his director compatriots, he chose to remain in Sweden but made plans for an English-language and large US-based production with major international actors.[33] These plans were abruptly canceled. Instead, Moodysson made a small-budget film, *A Hole in My Heart*, which is thematically focused on the global reach of the porn industry and the perils of Western consumerism.[34] With its thin plot and dialogue in Swedish, the film features four characters confined to a small and mundane 1970s apartment for a 24-hour amateur porn shoot, during which they philosophize, copulate, confess, and gorge on junk food. Shot with a handheld digital video camera, *A Hole in My Heart* is a bare bones production reminiscent of inexpensive reality television or made-at-home pornography. The film includes a montage of detailed and explicit scenes of genital and open-heart surgery that are unrelated to the plot, as well as scenes of violence and sexual abuse. It is a testament to Moodysson's auteur stature and Memfis' clout and marketing strategies that the film received coproduction funding from multiple agencies and that it was selected to screen at the Berlin International Film Festival and subsequently released for theater distribution in the United Kingdom, the United States, and the Nordic countries.[35]

The conditions for production of this film were experimental on a number of levels. Moodysson explains, "I felt like traditional film shoots did not allow for experimental creativity; they become too strict and too hierarchical. I wanted a smaller team and a different process. And I wanted the film to be a document about the process, the experiment in itself. And *A Hole in My Heart* is the most experimental of my films."[36] From script development to filming and final editing, the film is the result of a small team's close and dynamic collaboration.[37] *A Hole in My Heart* is the first film in which Moodysson has extensively operated the camera.[38] "I wanted to handle the camera myself. I think I had always been a little jealous of the photo-team, because they are physically present in the scene, when it is being shot. And if you think about the B-photo: the transition in focus is material and physical, the micro-seconds involved; that is the B-photographer's fingerprint in the final film.[39] I wanted my own fingerprint to be there, physically, materially, in *A Hole in My Heart*."[40] The materiality of the medium Moodysson appears interested in exploring also extended to the situations surrounding the filming. Behind-the-scenes reports state that the actors actually had sex on screen, while the physical location—an anonymous apartment in Trollhättan—is described by Moodysson as crucial to the experiment. In some ways, he says, "All my films begin with locations. It is as if places are characters in my films."[41] Though the cast and crew did not live on set, they stayed in the same apartment complex in neighboring apartments for four weeks. This was challenging to everyone involved, Moodysson adds, but a requisite part of the experimental process.[42]

Moodysson's subsequent film, *Container* (2006), and the art exhibit that accompanied it continue along the thematic trajectory established in *Lilya 4-ever* and *A Hole in My Heart*. It, too, is an investigation of abuse and confinement.[43] The later film explores transgender entrapment and includes an allegorical gesture to the soul's entrapment in the body, or it could be seen as an allusion to Christ in the tomb. *Container* is also experimental in terms of production design and filming location. Set partly in an apartment filled with trash and discarded items, *Container* was also shot at a giant trash heap in Romania and in the abandoned and contaminated no-go zone at the nuclear power plant in Chernobyl, the site of the accident in 1986 that spread poisonous radioactive matter across Russia and Northern Europe. In *Container* Moodysson reinvestigates his fascination with post-Soviet contemporary life as a life of ruins, which he presents so clearly in *Lilya 4-ever*. *Container* brings the social and political into tension with a conflicted human interiority, particularly in terms of transgender identity. Filmed in grainy black and white on 16 mm with 1960s Bolex cameras, this is a film in the tradition of 1970s art film. *Container* continues Moodysson's interest in challenging both conventional gender roles and heteronormative sexuality. It screened at the Berlin Film Festival in 2006 and in limited cinema release in Sweden later that year to very mixed reviews.[44]

A distinguishing feature of Lukas Moodysson's career has been its diversity in terms of film topics, genres, and styles. Amidst this diversity, Moodysson has maintained certain focal points in his cinematic oeuvre, which include a thematic emphasis on gender and sexuality, the inclusion of children's and outsiders' perspectives, and explicit interest in representing location. Moodysson's subsequent film, the big-budget international film project *Mammoth*, continues exploring these interests in new ways.[45] The plot's global scope takes on the gendered implications of neoliberalism and globalization. The film addresses Western upper-class parenting, third-world migrant women's labor, child prostitution, and the inequitable social and economic relations between the United States and Southeast Asia. The narrative interweaves three separate story lines and was shot in New York City, Thailand, the Philippines, and Trollhättan, Sweden. The international cast means that dialogue is in English, Thai, and Tagalog. Like many of Moodysson's films, *Mammoth* includes key roles by adolescents and young adults whose perspicuity and vulnerability are set against adult pretensions and falsehood. The plot strand set in New York City emphasizes the replacement of the mother's role, as Philippine nanny Gloria (Marife Necesito) cares for young Jackie (Sophie Nyweide), and the guilt this produces in her mother, the hard-working emergency room surgeon Ellen Vidales (Michelle Williams). The plot strand set in Thailand centers on Vidales' software-developer husband's (Gael García Bernal) escapist adventure to the beach with a young prostitute and mother of an infant, Cookie (Run Srinikornchot). The plot strand set in the Philippines addresses the troubles of Gloria's children Salvador (Jan Nicdao) and Manuel (Martin Delos Santos) left under the care of their grandmother, including a slide into child prostitution. Gloria leaves New York at the end of the film to return home to care for her sons. These are recognizable plot strands and themes from Moodysson's oeuvre, yet the film offers no clear moral resolution and no happy ending. At the end of the film, the Vidales simply acknowledge with detachment: "We'll have to get a new nanny."

There is a big step from low-budget *Container* with a production cost of about SEK 3 million (about 400,000 USD) and explicitly designed to be a small and narrowly-focused art film to the major international production *Mammoth*. Moodysson's close relationship with producer Lars Jönsson at Memfis Film, and its ability to get Moodysson funding, provided a foundation for the filmmaker's artistic freedom. *Mammoth* production began in the fall of 2007, and release was scheduled for September 2008; it eventually premiered at the Berlin Film Festival in February 2009. Despite the massive investment by Memfis (it is the company's most expensive film) and other funding agencies, including SFI, which awarded it the single largest sum of production support in Swedish film history, SEK 11 million (about 1.5 million USD), the film did not recuperate costs.[46] By the end of 2009, 270,000 cinema tickets had been sold, and the film received only limited theatrical release outside the Nordic countries, though it has been distributed worldwide in the form of TV, DVD, or digital pay-per-view.[47] The reception of *Mammoth* in Sweden was ambivalent and internationally was lukewarm.[48]

Unlike *A Hole in My Heart* and *Container*, *Mammoth* is not explicitly experimental. It is the first of Moodysson's films that can be called conventionally beautiful; its captivating landscape depiction is a contributing factor. The cinematography of Marcel Zyskind is rich in visual detail, expertly lit, and employs slow and steady camera movements that emphasize the geographical distinctiveness of each location—the New York City streetscape is contrasted with a gorgeous beach in Thailand; an enormous trash heap in the Philippines is juxtaposed with Bangkok air pollution. *Mammoth* employs the broad projection aspect ratio of traditional cinemascope (2.35:1). Moodysson chose this format as a way to combine numerous close-ups with rich background details in order to portray individuals against an epic background.[49] Michal Leszczylowski's careful editing is based on thematic and visual continuity. Moodysson indicates that these are strategic choices. "I wanted this film to be beautiful," says Moodysson. "I wanted to contrast its melancholy and sadness with beautiful cinematography. In contrast to *Lilya 4-ever* and *A Hole in My Heart* I sought to emphasize the beauty of this earth. I wanted to portray pain and evil against a visually stunning and expansive backdrop."[50] Moodysson's characteristic ambivalence also motivated his choice of photographer. This visual impetus is, perhaps, also part of the film's perceived weakness. Its beauty, near A-list cast, and conventional big-budget aesthetics confound a viewer expecting Moodysson's experimental approach and social and political commentary.

Recurring aspects of Moodysson's films are that they tend to focus on adolescents or (young) women protagonists. The narratives challenge the boundaries of the small town (*Show Me Love*) or the Swedish nation-state (*Together*) and in later films move toward questioning transnational movements and globalization paradigms (*Lilya 4-ever*, *A Hole in My Heart*, *Mammoth*). These films foreground characters caught in human trafficking, the global porn industry, and prostitution. Moodysson appears invested in the idea of authenticity, but as his films move further away from the Swedish national context (both in plot and production) his search for authenticity as part of a vehicle for manifesting the ambiguity inherent to cinematic works in the twenty-first century. The director's professed interest in authenticity, including in production design, remains a strong driving force throughout his career. Yet, as this book has shown, Moodysson's representation of gender, sexuality, space, and location is never straightforward or ideologically clear-cut; the director's interest in cinematic experimentation adds a layer of complexity to the overt content of his films. As such, Lukas Moodysson may be dedicated to an idea and ideology of cinematic authenticity and simultaneously be a practitioner of aesthetic ambivalence.

Festival Screenings and Awards

SHOW ME LOVE FESTIVAL AND INTERNERNATIONAL SCREENINGS, 1999–2009[1]

1999
Atlantic Film Festival, Halifax
Barcelona International Gay and Lesbian Film Festival
BUFF: The International Children and Young People's Film Festival
Cape Town International Film Festival
Cork Film Festival
Edinburgh International Film Festival
European Queer Film and Arts Alliance London
Filmfest Ludwigsburg
Ghent Film Festival
Gothenburg International Film Festival
Jerusalem Film Festival
Karlovy Vary International Film Festival
Lilla Filmfestivalen, Båstad Sweden
Ljubljana International Film Festival
Macedonia Film Festival

Molodist Kiev International Film Festival
Montreal International Queer Film and Video Festival
New Zealand International Film Festival Wellington
Norwegian International Film Festival Haugesund
Pusan International Film Festival
Rio International Film Festival
Rotterdam International Film Festival
San Francisco International Lesbian & Gay Film Festival
Seattle International Film Festival
Stockholm Film Festival
Sydney Film Festival
Toronto International Film Festival
Valencia Film Festival
Vancouver International Film Festival
Viennale, Austria
Warszaw Film Festival

2000
Bangkok International Film Festival
Hong Kong Lesbian and Gay Film Festival
International Istanbul Film Festival
Kolkata Film Festival [Calcutta]
Lisbon Gay and Lesbian Film Festival
Madrid International LGTB Film Festival
Mardi Gras Queer Screen Film Festival, Australia
Melbourne Queer Film Festival
New Delhi European Union Film Festival
Out in Africa: South African Gay and Lesbian Film Festival
Rouen Nordic Film Festival
Up-and-coming International Film Festival Hannover
Scandinavian Film Week in Paris

2001
Chinese Queer Women Film Festival
Havana Film Festival

2002
Gothenburg International Film Festival
International Youth Film and Video Festival, Covilha, Portugal

2003
Kristiansand International Children's Film Festival
Transilvania International Film Festival

2004
Pride International Film Festival, Manila, Philippines
Torino GLBT Film Festival

2005
Sofia International Film Festival

2006
Berlin International Film Festival, screened in Teddy Retro

2007
San Sebastian Film Festival

2009
Copenhagen World Out Games
Florence International Film Festival [Moodysson retrospective]
Oulu International Children's Film Festival
São Paulo International Film Festival

SHOW ME LOVE AWARDS, (1999)[2]

Amanda Award for best foreign feature film (Haugesund, Norway)
Atlantic Film Festival: Best International Feature Award
Berlin International Film Festival: Teddy Award for best feature film
European Film Awards: nominated for best film
Flanders International Film Festival: Student Jury Award to Lukas Moodysson
Guldbagge Awards (Sweden's equivalent to the Oscars): best film, best direction, best screenplay, and best actress to Alexandra Dahlström and Rebecka Liljeberg
Karlovy Vary International Film Festival: Audience Award, Don Quijote Award, Special Prize of the Jury
Lilla filmfestivalen i Båstad: Bo Widerberg Film Award
London Film Festival: Sutherland Trophy and special mention to Lukas Moodysson
Macedonian Film Festival: Brothers Manaki Award, Special Jury Award to Ulf Brantås, cinematographer
Molodist International Film Festival: Best Film Award, FIPRESCI Prize, Youth Jury Award
Rotterdam International Film Festival: MovieZone Award
Valencia International Film Festival: Golden Moon of Valencia—Cinema Jove

Notes

1. MOODYSSON'S CONTEXTS

1. Michele Aaron, "New Queer Cinema: An Introduction," in *New Queer Cinema: A Critical Reader*, ed. Michele Aaron (Edinburgh: Edinburgh University Press, 2004), 8.
2. Ingmar Bergman, *Bergmans 1900-Tal: En hyllning till svensk film, från Victor Sjöström till Lukas Moodysson*, ed. Gunnar Bergdahl (Göteborg: Göteborg Film Festival, 2000); Leif Furhammar, *Filmen i Sverige: En Historia i Tio Kapitel och en Fortsättning*, 3rd ed. (Stockholm: Dialogos, 2003), 367. All translations into English are my own, unless otherwise noted.
3. Cyrill Hellman, *Stefan Jarl: En intervjubok* (Stockholm: Kartago, 2008), 284; Jannike Åhlund, *New Cinema in Sweden* (Stockholm: Swedish Institute, 2002), 19.
4. Matthew Sweet, "Bought and Sold? Lukas Moodysson's Acclaimed New Film *Lilya 4-ever*," *The Independent* (London), March 28, 2003. Other representative examples include Per Dabelsteen, "Interview: En Rejse Fra og til Helvede," *Politiken* (Copenhagen), September 27, 2002, who writes that Moodysson may be "the new Bergman"; see also Antoine Jacob, "Lukas Moodysson, cinéaste

citoyen," *Le Monde* (Paris), April 21, 2003; and Tom de Castella, "Revival—Tom de Castella charts how Swedish film finally cast off Bergman's shadow," *New Statesman*, September 15, 2003.

5   Some of Moodysson's later poetry collections include *Mellan sexton och tjugosex* [*Between sixteen and twenty-six*] (Stockholm: Wahlström och Widstrand, 2001); *Vad gör jag här: en dikt* [*What am I doing here: A poem*] (Stockholm: Wahlström och Widstrand, 2002); and *Apo Kryp Hos* (Stockholm: Wahlström och Widstrand, 2006). He gives as sources of inspiration Bruno K. Öijer, Lars Norén, Gunnar Ekelöf, and Michael Strunge, according to Kevin Conroy Scott, "Lukas Moodysson: *Together*," in *Screenwriters' Masterclass: Screenwriters Talk About Their Greatest Movies*, ed. Kevin Conroy Scott (London: Faber and Faber, 2005), 247. His most recent novels are *Döden & Co.* (Stockholm: Wahlström och Widstrand, 2011) and *En vacker sjuk plats* (Stockholm: Wahlström och Widstrand, 2012).

6   Scott, "Lukas Moodysson: *Together*," 259. All quotes from dialogue or script in Moodysson's films, unless otherwise noted, are culled from the English subtitles provided on Memfis Box-set of DVDs (Stockholm, 2009).

7   I explore the claims of and interest in authenticity in these two Moodysson books, including as they pertain to the author's interest in youth and to the filmmaker's practices, elsewhere in my scholarship.

8   Mats Weman, "Pastor Moodyssons Bekännelser," *Nöjesguiden*, September 9, 2000; Malena Janson, "Sjuttiotalet är en rolig värld att dyka ner i," *Svenska Dagbladet*, August 16, 2000.

9   Weman, "Pastor."

10 Scott, "Lukas Moodysson: *Together*," 264.

11 Åhlund, *New Cinema in Sweden*, 20.

12 Reversed film stock yields a positive image on the original, which can be projected directly. Negative film requires processing to a positive copy. This process is discussed more fully in chapter 2.

13 See list of interviews at the end of this book.

14 Scott, "Lukas Moodysson: *Together*," 245–46.
15 *Det spelar ingen roll var blixtarna slår ner* [*It does not matter where the lightning hits*] (Stockholm: Wahlström och Widstrand, 1987); *Och andra dikter* [*And Other Poems*] (Stockholm: Wahlström och Widstrand, 1988); *Evangelium enligt Lukas Moodysson* [*The Gospel According to Lukas Moodysson*] (Stockholm: Wahlström och Widstrand, 1989); *Kött* [*Meat*] (Stockholm: Wahlström och Widstrand, 1991); and the autobiographical novel *Vitt blod* [*White Blood*] (Stockholm: Wahlström och Widstrand, 1990).
16 Stephen Lowenstein, "Lukas Moodysson: *Show Me Love*," in *My First Move Take Two: Ten Celebrated Directors Talk About Their First Film*, ed. Stephen Lowenstein (New York: Pantheon, 2008), 204.
17 Lukas Moodysson, research interview; see also Scott, "Lukas Moodysson: *Together*," 249; and ibid., 204–5.
18 Mattias Göransson, "Efter Fucking Åmål," *DN Lördag Söndag*, August 19, 2000; Moodysson, research interview.
19 Fiona Morrow, "Cool Hand Lukas," *The Independent* (London), July 6, 2001.
20 Moodysson, research interview.
21 Lukas Moodysson, "Ett pressmeddelande," Trollhättan, October 18, 1999.
22 Moodysson, research interview.
23 Lukas Moodysson, *En uppgörelse i den undre världen* [*Settlement in the Under World*] (Stockholm: Dramatiska institutet, 1996). The film was screened on Swedish television as part of a series featuring graduating new directors, but was otherwise met with critical and public silence.
24 Lukas Moodysson, *Talk* (*Bara prata lite*), in *Memfis Shorts*, Memfis DVD, directed by Lukas Moodysson (1997; 2009). The Memfis approach to film production is unusual if not unique in the contemporary Swedish film industry, as multiple experts, journalists, and professionals affirm. See also Per Andersson, "Memfis, Stockholm,"

Teknik och Människa (June 2005): 8–9. Memfis works closely with its directors, including doing pilot films with emerging ones before proceeding to full features intended for theatrical release. Moodysson's *Talk* and Maria Blom's *Fishy* (Memfis, 2008) are prominent examples; Josef Fares also did a Memfis pilot before *Jalla! Jalla!* (Memfis, 2000).

25 Moodysson, research interview.
26 Lars Jönsson, research interview.
27 As a point of contrast, Yellowbird Productions (based on a partnership formed in 2002 by Danish producer Ole Søndberg and Swedish writer Henning Mankell) seeks explicitly to capitalize on best-seller literature. Their company slogan is "We turn bestsellers into blockbusters," Yellowbird Productions, http://www.yellowbird.se (accessed November 13, 2009).
28 Jönsson, research interview. The Memfis mentality seems also to have influenced several emerging players in the Swedish film industry, including producer Jesper Kurlandsky, director Alexandra Dahlström (who played Elin in *Show Me Love*), and Garagefilm producers Rebecka Lafrenz and Mimmi Spång. Kurlandsky, for example, has worked for Memfis, including with research and production, for all of Moodysson's films since *Together*. He has since produced Jesper Ganslandt's internationally well-received *The Ape [Apan]* (Fasad, 2009). Dahlström won the Stockholm Film Festival's 2008 prize for emerging directors and recently released her third short film as a director, *Because the Night* (Bob Film, 2009).
29 Jönsson, research interview.
30 Roger Wilson, "Sista Föreställningen," *Fokus* 35 (2006): 24–33.
31 Michal Leszczylowski, research interview.
32 Janson, "Sjuttiotalet."
33 Moodysson, research interview.
34 Scott, "Lukas Moodysson: *Together*," 256.
35 David Noh, "Hardcore Spiritualism: Sweden's Lukas Moodysson

36 Explores Personal Vision in *Lilya 4-Ever*," *Film Journal International* 106, no. 5 (2003): 18–20.
36 Göransson, "Efter Fucking Åmål." *Show Me Love* has been adapted for the stage and produced in Germany, Iceland, and Finland; *Lilya 4-Ever* has been adapted for the stage and produced in Germany and Spain; *Mammoth* has been adapted for the stage and produced in The Netherlands.
37 Moodysson, research interview. See also Carl Johan de Geer, "Om en märklig inspelning," *Aftonbladet*, August 27, 2000.
38 Moodysson, research interview.
39 Ibid.
40 Alexandra Dahlström, research interview.
41 Scott, "Lukas Moodysson: *Together*," 263; Moodysson, research interview.
42 Moodysson, research interview.
43 Mette Hjort, *Small Nation, Global Cinema: The New Danish Cinema* (Minneapolis: University of Minnesota Press, 2005), 1–66; Mette Hjort, *Lone Scherfig's* Italian for Beginners (Seattle: University of Washington Press, 2010).
44 Göransson, "Efter Fucking Åmål."
45 Ibid., 9.
46 Ibid., 9.
47 Gabriel Axel, *Babette's Feast* [*Babettes gæstebud*] (Orion Classics, 1988).
48 Cf. Xan Brooks, "Dirty Business," *The Guardian*, January 4, 2005; Lowenstein, "Lukas Moodysson: *Show Me Love*," 203. Moodysson does acknowledge Bergman's "formidable presence" and has indicated that he feels close to the character Alexander in *Fanny and Alexander* [*Fanny och Alexander*] (Svensk filmindustri, 1982); cf. Lukas Moodysson, "My desperate teenagers," interview with Lukas Moodysson, August 30, 2002, www.cineurope.org.

2. THE AMBIVALENCE OF *SHOW ME LOVE*

1   Laura Mulvey, "Visual Pleasure and Narrative Cinema," in *The Feminism and Visual Culture Reader*, ed. Amelia Jones (London: Routledge, 2003), 44–53.
2   Stephen Lowenstein, "Lukas Moodysson: *Show Me Love*," in *My First Move Take Two: Ten Celebrated Directors Talk About Their First Film*, ed. Stephen Lowenstein (New York: Pantheon, 2008), 210–11.
3   Lukas Moodysson, research interview.
4   Alexandra Keining's romantic drama *With Every Heartbeat* (Kyss mig, 2011; Lebox Produktion) is the second Swedish feature to concentrate on a developing lesbian relationship.
5   *Show Me Love* was, in fact, the first major critical and economic success coproduced by the emerging regional film center Film i Väst in Trollhättan. This film subsequently helped propel Film i Väst into becoming one of the most important coproduction agencies and filming locations in Sweden and Scandinavia during the following decade (see chapter 3 of this book).
6   Though there is no explicit sex scene between the two young women, there is a masturbation scene, during which Agnes looks at a picture of Elin. I return to discuss this scene later.
7   *Svensk filmdatabas*, http://www.sfi.se/en-gb/Swedish-film-database/ (accessed April 12, 2010). *Svensk filmdatabas*, administered by Svenska Filminstitutet, provides a wealth of information about films made in Sweden, including ticket sales. All information about film specifics and ticket sales in this book is culled from this database. Its information overlaps partly with that provided in *The Internet Movie Database*, http://www.imdb.com/ (accessed April 12, 2010).
8   Reviews were printed in a majority of Swedish daily papers on October 23, 1998, the day the film premiered. For representative reviews, see Johan Croneman, "Längtan bort förlamar och frigör," *Dagens*

Nyheter, October 23, 1998; Bo Ludvigsson, "Starkt och modigt om att finna sitt liv," *Svenska Dagbladet*, October 23, 1998; Annika Gustafsson, "Hem till byn," *Sydsvenska dagbladet*, October 23, 1998; Jonas Cramby, "Fucking Great," *Expressen*, October 23, 1998; and Jan-Olov Andersson, "En fucking skit-bra film," *Aftonbladet*, October 23, 1998.

9   Charlotta Denward, research interview.

10 As such, the title corresponds to an international popularization of queer theory at the end of the 1990s, particularly Judith Butler's concept of performativity. See Judith Butler, *Gender Trouble: Feminism and the Subversion of Identity* (London: Routledge, 1990) and *Bodies That Matter: On the Discursive Limits of "Sex"* (London: Routledge, 1993); see also Teresa de Lauretis' insistence on gay and lesbian sexuality as cultural forms independent from heterosexuality: Teresa de Lauretis, "Queer Theory: Lesbian and Gay Studies: An Introduction," *Differences: A Journal of Feminist Cultural Studies* 3, no. 2 (1991): iii–xviii; and Eve Kosofsky Sedgwick's argument about western modernity as hinged on a binary opposition between homosexuality and heterosexuality: Eve Kosofsky Sedgwick, *Epistemology of the Closet* 2nd ed. (Berkeley: University of California Press, 2008 [1990]).

11 As referenced by Kerry Mallan, "Feeling a Little Queer? Performing Lesbian Desire and Identity in Youth Texts," in *Seriously Playful: Genre, Performance and Text*, ed. Kerry Mallan and Sharyn Pearce (Flaxton, Queensland: Post Pressed, 2004), 116.

12 Lars Jönsson, research interview.

13 Karin Thunberg, "Vart tog deras lesbiska kärlek vägen?" *Svenska Dagbladet*, December 12, 1998; See also Linda Norrman Skugge, "Varför tiger recensenterna om lesbisk kärlek/," *Expressen*, December 12, 1998.

14 This reception trajectory has a significant counterpart in the reception of Henrik Ibsen's *A Doll's House* over a century earlier (1879), which divided along similar lines. Because the play is about a woman, it can-

not be universal; or, it is universal because it is not *really* about Nora as a woman, but about her as a human being. Like Ibsen, Moodysson tells stories about women in the modern age, and while conceived more than a century apart, these works strike similar chords about the function of gender.

15 These films include Brian Gilbert's *Wilde* (British Broadcasting Corporation, 1997), Todd Haynes' *Velvet Goldmine* (Miramax, 1998), and Clint Eastwood's *Midnight in the Garden of Good and Evil* (Malpaso Productions, 1997). Tiina Rosenberg outlines the critical reception in detail in the article "Det Nya Lukas-Evangeliet: Om Det Heteronormativa Mottagandet Av Fucking Åmål," *Lambda nordica* 6, no. 4 (2000): 23–36; see also Birgitta Tollan Driesel, "Tystnadens historia," *Bang: Feministisk kulturtidskrift* 1 (1991): 30–33; and Fanny Ambjörnsson, "Vem forskar om Agnes och Elin?" *Bang: Feministisk kulturtidskrift* 1 (1991): 33–38.

16 Photographer Elisabeth Ohlson's exhibit *Ecce Homo* caused particular controversy and debate when it was exhibited in Uppsala cathedral in fall 1998, the same time as the release of *Show Me Love* in Sweden. The images include nudes and sexualized situations. Elisabeth Ohlson, photography exhibit, 1998, http://www.ohlson.se/utstallningar_ecce.htm.

17 Cf. Jenny Svenberg, "Tack Gud att jag är lesbisk: Om homosexualitet," in *Fittstim*, ed. Linda Norrman Skugge, Belinda Olsson, and Brita Zilg (Stockholm: Bokförlaget DN, 1999), 102–11.

18 Moodysson and Alexandra Dahlström, research interviews.

19 Don Kulick, ed., *Queersverige* (Stockholm: Natur och Kultur, 2005); Tiina Rosenberg, "Det Nya Lukas-Evangeliet: Om Det Heteronormativa Mottagandet Av Fucking Åmål," 23–36.

20 Karin Nikolajevna, for example, argues that the film's structure mirrors a type of *Romeo and Juliet* plot. Karin Nikolajevna, "Fucking Åmål—Varför En Succé? En Litteraturvetares Syn på Saken," in *Talandets Lust Och Vånda*, ed. Britt Backlund (Lund: Studentlittera-

tur, 2000), 89–101. Jenny Björklund makes a strong case for the film as a traditionally schematic Hollywood romance. Jenny Björklund, "Queering the Small Town; Lukas Moodysson's Film *Show Me Love*," *Women's Studies* 39, no. 1 (2010): 37–51; see also Kerry Mallan, "Feeling a Little Queer? Performing Lesbian Desire and Identity in Youth Texts," 113–21; Sven Hansell, "Du Är Inte Normal! Kön, Norm Och Frihet i Lukas Moodyssons Filmer," *Kvinnovetenskaplig tidskrift* 25, no. 1/2 (2004): 99–112.

21 Björklund, "Queering the Small Town," 38.
22 Technically, while the car is stalled, they seem to think they are on their way to Stockholm. This may be a key reason why they kiss. Their escape is actually thwarted following the kiss, and their remaining in Åmål constitutes a new obstacle.
23 The Dogme 95, "Manifesto" and "Vow of Chastity" are reprinted in *Purity and Provocation: Dogma 95*, ed. Mette Hjort and Scott MacKenzie (London: British Film Institute, 2003), 199–200; their "Introduction" provides an excellent overview.
24 Moodysson and Jönsson, research interviews.
25 Jönsson, research interview.
26 *Show Me Love* was filmed on Kodak's slower reverse stock, 125 or 160 ASA, according to Brantås (although he cannot recall exactly which speed), which is a Kodak Ektachrome process.
27 Ulf Brantås, research interview.
28 Moodysson, research interview.
29 Jönsson, research interview.
30 Moodysson and Brantås, research interviews.
31 Moodysson, research interview.
32 Ibid.
33 Ibid.
34 Ibid.
35 Ibid.
36 Moodysson and Michael Leszczylowski, research interviews.

37 Brantås, research interview.
38 See Mette Hjort, *Small Nation, Global Cinema: The New Danish Cinema* (Minneapolis: University of Minnesota Press, 2005), 34–48; Trevor Elkington, "Costumes, Adolescence, and Dogma: Nordic Film and American Distribution," in *Transnational Cinema in a Global North: Nordic Cinema in Transition*, ed. Andrew Nestingen and Trevor Elkington (Detroit, MI: Wayne State University Press, 2002), 31–54.
39 Brantås and Leszczylowski, research interviews.
40 Much has been written on this issue, both about the presumed opposition between the Widerberg generation of realist directors and the fact that Bergman's films of the 1950s and 1960s were generally not well received or popular in Sweden, so that his legacy was first established in Europe and North America—see for example Peter Cowie, *Ingmar Bergman: A Critical Biography* (New York: Charles Scribner's Sons, 1982), 341–42.
41 Stephen Lowenstein, "Lukas Moodysson: *Show Me Love*," 203; Ingmar Bergman, *Bergmans 1900-Tal: En Hyllning Till Svensk Film, Från Victor Sjöström Till Lukas Moodysson*, ed. Gunnar Bergdahl (Göteborg: Göteborg Film Festival, 2000).
42 See Andrew K. Nestingen, *Crime and Fantasy in Scandinavia: Fiction, Film, and Social Change* (Seattle: University of Washington Press, 2008), 107–10; Olof Hedling, "'Sveriges Mest Kända Korvkiosk': Om regionaliseringen av svensk film," in *Solskenslandet: Svensk Film på 2000-Talet*, ed. Erik Hedling and Ann-Kristin Wallengren (Malmö: Atlantis, 2006), 44; and Mary P. Wood, *Contemporary European Cinema* (London: Hodder Arnold, 2007), 90. The tension in *Show Me Love* between innovation and convention is also evident in the sense that Moodysson belongs to a significant group of emerging European directors in the 1990s who tell stories that relate to viewers across age, sex, and other demographic lines and are not opaque exercises in auteur experimentation.

43 Björklund, 42.
44 Brantås, research interview.
45 Gwendolyn Audrey Foster, "Feminist Theory and the Performance of Lesbian Desire in *Persona*," in *Ingmar Bergman's "Persona,"* ed. Lloyd Michaels (Cambridge: Cambridge University Press, 1999), 130, 132, 133.
46 Ibid., 137.
47 Ibid., 136.
48 Maaret Koskinen, *Ingmar Bergman's "The Silence": Pictures in the Typewriter, Writings on the Screen* (Seattle: University of Washington Press, 2009). Erik Hedling, "Breaking the Swedish Sex Barrier: Painful Lustfulness in Ingmar Bergman's *The Silence*," *Film International* 36, no. 6 (2008): 17–27.
49 Another interesting example of Moodysson's deliberate ambivalence is Jessica's physical assault of Elin, when she thinks her younger sister has pursued her own boyfriend for herself. This assault can, however, also be seen as Jessica's reaction to understanding Elin's implicit acknowledgment of lesbian attraction, in which case the violence becomes both heteronormative and, possibly, an act of incestuous jealousy. But this rationale is also tinged with a strange kind of incestuous potential (and sibling rivalry), which extends to the possible transfer of Jessica's affections to Johan at the end of the film. It all seems to question the foundations of heteronormative practices within a closed community; are they to safeguard against both incest and same-sex desire?
50 Björklund, 41.
51 Foster, "Feminist Theory and the Performance of Lesbian Desire in *Persona*," 139, 141.
52 Humiliation is "perhaps the nucleus of Bergman's artistic philosophy." Jörn Donner, *The Films of Ingmar Bergman: From Torment to All These Women*, trans. Holger Lundbergh (New York: Dover, 1972), 100.

53 Rosenberg has discussed this legacy in a number of different venues. See for example Rosenberg, "Det Nya Lukas-Evangeliet," 23–36.
54 Leslie Feinberg, *Stone Butch Blues: A Novel* (Ann Arbor, MI: Firebrand Books, 1993).
55 Moodysson, research interview.
56 Dahlström, research interview.
57 "Skål för Åmål," *Expressen*, October 23, 1998.
58 Broder Daniel, "Underground," performed by Broder Daniel (Jimmy Fun Music/EMI Music, 1998). Moodysson attests in a research interview to his long-term interest in the indie-rock band Broder Daniel. He also directed the band's first video to the song "Work." See Martin Norberg and Klas Ekman, *Broder Daniel: When We Were Winning* (Stockholm: Telegram Förlag, 2009), 64.
59 Nikolajevna, however, argues that this scene fixes the characters in a childlike and non-eroticized realm. Karin Nikolajevna, "Fucking Åmål—Varför En Succé?" 89–101.
60 The mise-en-scène of Elin's room includes a big beefcake poster of a shirtless young man over the dresser at camera left; Agnes sits next to it while waiting for Elin to come in. When Elin moves toward the bed, we see a heart-shaped balloon on the wall that reads, "Hugs & Kisses"; while they are seated on the bed, we see a smaller glamour headshot of another apparently shirtless young man, an image of Winnie the Pooh, and a couple of posters with some kind of writing on them. Winnie the Pooh wears the same color top as Elin, and both he and Elin have the same yellowish color due to the lighting of the scene. Pooh is also drinking from a honey pot, as the girls are drinking from their respective glasses. The phrase *honey pot* used to be American slang for vagina. There is a similar connotation in Swedish. This scene's emphasis on fluid, overflow, and orality is actually quite sensual and perhaps specifically appropriate for the enactment of lesbian desire. The mise-en-scène characteristically mixes what appears obviously heteronormative (posters of men) with the suggestively lesbian (Pooh's honey).

61 Moodysson and Brantås, research interviews.
62 Harry Benshoff and Sean Griffin, "General Introduction," in *Queer Cinema: The Film Reader* (New York: Routledge, 2005), 6. The authors quote Richard Dyer and note that "Carl Theodor Dreyer's Mikael (Universum Film, 1924) filmed in Germany a few years later, was drawn from the same source novel." Richard Dyer with Julianne Pidduck, *Now You See It: Studies in Lesbian and Gay Film*, 2nd ed. (London: Routledge, 2003 [1990]), 6.
63 Cited in Michele Aaron, "New Queer Cinema: An Introduction," in *New Queer Cinema: A Critical Reader* (Edinburgh: Edinburgh University Press, 2004), 3–14.
64 Ibid., 3.
65 See for example Clare Whatling, *Screen Dream: Fantasising Lesbians in Film* (Manchester: Manchester University Press, 1997), 82; Jamie Stuart, *Performing Queer Female Identity on Screen: A Critical Analysis of Five Recent Films* (n.p.: McFarland & Company, 2008), 54–59.
66 Ibid., 8; Björklund, 38.
67 Michael Bronski, "Positive Images and the Coming Out Film," Screen 26, no. 1 (2000): 23, 26; see also Julianne Pidduck, "After 1980: Margins and Mainstreams" in *Now You See It: Studies in Lesbian and Gay Film*, 2nd ed., ed. Richard Dyer with Julianne Pidduck (London: Routledge, 2003), 280–82.
68 Timothy Shary, *Teen Movies: American Youth on Screen* (London: Wallflower Press, 2005), 53; see also 54–67.
69 Jeffrey P. Dennis, *Queering Teen Culture: All-American Boys and Same Sex Desire in Film and Television* (New York: Harrington Park Press, 2006), 149–87.
70 For a list of brat packers, see Dennis, *Queering Teen Culture*, 149–51.
71 Moodysson, research interview.
72 Moodysson, research interview.

3. THE GEOGRAPHY OF *SHOW ME LOVE*

1. In domestic markets of the late 1990s, "Nordic films account for only 20 percent of domestic ticket sales, with Hollywood taking most of the rest." Trevor Elkington and Andrew Nestingen, "Introduction. Transnational Nordic Cinema," in *Transnational Cinema in a Global North: Nordic Cinema in Transition*, ed. Andrew Nestingen and Trevor Elkington (Detroit, MI: Wayne State University Press, 2002), 7.

2. An incomplete list of countries and release dates is available at http://www.imdb.com/title/tt0150662/releaseinfo#akas (accessed January 10, 2010). This information has been supplemented by documents from the Swedish Film Institute and Lars Jönsson at Memfis film.

3. Coverage (review and interviews) in the influential Danish daily newspaper *Politiken* is especially positive. See Liselotte Michelsen, "Teenage-land Retur," *Politiken* (Copenhagen), March 19, 1999; Hans Jørgen Møller, "Hjertekvaler i Sovebyen," *Politiken* (Copenhagen), March 12, 1999.

4. See reviews by Anthony Quinn, "The Arts," *The Independent* (London), March 3, 2000; Philip French, "Swedish teenagers fall in love in the most surprising places...," *The Observer* (London), March 5, 2000; Stephen Applebaum, "Swedehearts," *The New Scotsman*, February 26, 2000.

5. See Jacques Mandelbaum, "Fucking Åmål: Film Suédois de Lukas Moodysson," *Le Monde* (Paris), June 7, 2000; Hans-Dieter Seidel, "Raus aus Åmål," *Frankfurter Allgemeine Zeitung*, December 4, 1999; "Raus aus Åmål," *Der Spiegel*, November 29, 1999; Oliver Fuchs, "Das Lange Warten auf die grosse Flatter," *Die Welt*, December 2, 1999; and Gwen Douget, "Lukas Moodysson, un poète devenu cinéaste," *Le Figaro*, June 7, 2000.

6. *Show Me Love* was reviewed by several of Canada's major newspapers. See Rick Groen, "Girl Meets Girl Story's Pitch-Perfect Hormone

Hell," *The Globe and Mail* (Canada), October 29, 1999; Bill Brownstein, "Show Me Love, not sex: A sensitively told Lesbian love story," *The Gazette* (Montreal), October, 30 1999; Bruce Kirkland, "Swedish Film Shows Us Love," *Toronto Sun*, October 1999; and Peter Howell, "Girl Meets Girl in Coming-of-Age Tale," *The Toronto Star*, October 29, 1999. A representative review from Australia is Paul Byrnes, "Girl Meets Girl in Teen Romance with a Twist," *Morning Herald* (Sydney), December 14, 2000.

7   Anita Gates, "In a Swedish Town, Girls Will Be Girls," *The New York Times*, October 15, 1999; David Ansen, "Teen Spleen," *Newsweek*, October 18, 1999. *Show Me Love* has screened at a number of US film festivals, including the 1999 Seattle International Film Festival (its first US screening), the Boulder Gay and Lesbian Film Festival (Colorado); Out Takes Dallas Lesbian and Gay Film Festival; Inside Out, Gay and Lesbian Film and Video Festival of Toronto; and Washington DC's Reel Affirmations (gay and lesbian film festival). In 2000, *Show Me Love* was featured at the following festivals: Filmfest DC; Puerto Rico Film Festival; North Carolina Gay and Lesbian Film Festival; in 2009 at Outfest, Los Angeles Gay and Lesbian Film Festival. Partial release information is available at http://www.imdb.com/title/tt0150662/releaseinfo#akas (accessed April 12, 2010), supplemented here by information from Memfis Film and the Swedish Film Institute.

8   For a complete list of film festival screenings and awards, see the section "Festival Screenings and Awards" in this book.

9   See discussion of this issue in chapter 2 of this book. See also Karin Thunberg, "Vart tog deras lesbiska kärlek vägen?" *Svenska Dagbladet*, December 12, 1998; Tiina Rosenberg, "Det Nya Lukas-Evangeliet, 23–36.

10 As Jannike Åhlund affirms: "Historically, the children's film has held a strong position in Sweden," at least partly because of the strong tradition of children's literature, including "copious narrative mate-

rial supplied to several generations of filmmakers by author Astrid Lindgren"; *New Cinema in Sweden* (Stockholm: Swedish Institute, 2002), 37. Cf. Malena Janson, "Elvis! Elvis!" in *The Cinema of Scandinavia*, ed. Tytti Soila (London: Wallflower, 2005), 171–79; Maaret Koskinen, "The Swedish Film of the Eighties and Nineties: A Critical Survey," in *Film in Sweden*, ed. Francesco Bono and Maaret Koskinen (Stockholm: Swedish Institute, 1996), 27–29.

11 Quinn, "The Arts."

12 Stephanie Reynolds, "Lesbian Love Story a High School Classic," *The Daily Yomiuri* (Tokyo), May 18, 2000.

13 Philip French, "Swedish teenagers fall in love in the most surprising places. . . ."

14 Groen, "Girl Meets Girl Story's Pitch-Perfect Hormone Hell"; Brownstein, "Show Me Love, Not Sex."

15 On box office statistics, see *Svensk filmdatabas*, Svenska Filminstitutet, http://www.sfi.se/en-gb/Swedish-film-database/ (accessed April 12, 2010).

16 David Ansen writes, "Teenage life is captured so naturally . . . that you might mistake it for a documentary"; "Teen Spleen," *Newsweek*, October 18, 1999. See also Byrnes, "Girl Meets Girl in Teen Romance with a Twist"; Groen, "Girl Meets Girl Story's Pitch-Perfect Hormone Hell."

17 Jay Stone, "Familiar Story Beautifully Told," *The Ottawa Citizen*, November 26, 1999; Peter Howell, "Girl Meets Girl in Coming-of-Age Tale"; Michelson, "Teenage-land Retur."

18 Sweden has ranked near the top of the global gender equity list for many years.

19 Cf. Linda Haverty Rugg, "Gender and Sex in Scandinavian Cinema as Screened in the American Mind," in *Bent: Gender and Sexuality in Contemporary Scandinavian Art*, ed. Whitney Chadwick (San Francisco: International Center for the Arts at San Francisco State University, 2006), 34–39; Erik Hedling, "Breaking the Swedish Sex

Barrier: Painful Lustfulness in Ingmar Bergman's *The Silence*," *Film International* 36, no. 6 (2008): 17–27; Jeff Werner, *Medelvägens estetik. Sverigebilder i USA*, vol. 2 (Hedemora: Gidlunds, 2008), 129–71.

20 Peter Howell writes that "Amal denotes not a person, but rather the faceless Swedish town where the film's youthful protagonists live with an impatience for adulthood"; "Girl Meets Girl in Coming-of-Age Tale." Jim Schembi writes about "the small, nowhere town of Amal"; "Fragile Teens handled without mockery," *The Age* (Melbourne), December 22, 2000. Fuchs labels it "verfluchtes, verdammtes, vermaledeites Amal"; "Das Lange Warten auf die grosse Flatter." See also "Fucking Amal," *Le Point* (Paris), June 2, 2000.

21 French, "Swedish teenagers fall in love in the most surprising places..."

22 For a full discussion of this scene, see chapter 2.

23 Early Swedish film also made use of location substitution. *The Outlaw and his Wife*, for example, is set in Iceland and shot in Northern Sweden.

Bo Florin discusses silent cinema's use of landscape in "Den nationella stilen. Studier i den svenska filmens guldålder" (PhD diss., Stockholm University, 1997), 81–84. Marina Dahlquist argues that Stiller and Sjöstrom were "great dramaturges of nature"; "Snow-White: The Aesthetic and Narrative Use of Snow in Swedish Silent Film," in *Nordic Explorations in Film Before 1930*, ed. John Fullerton and Jan Olsson (Sydney, Australia: John Libbey, 1999), 239.

24 Erik Hedling, "The Welfare State Depicted: Post-Utopian Landscapes in Ingmar Bergman's Films," in *Ingmar Bergman Revisited: Performance, Cinema, and the Arts*, ed. Maaret Koskinen (London: Wallflower, 2008), 182.

25 As Qvist suggests, the landscape is "our culture and our home"; see Per Olov Qvist, *Folkhemmets Bilder: Modernisering, Motstånd och Mentalitet i Den Svenska 30-Talsfilmen* (Lund: Arkiv, 1995), 288, as cited in and translated by Erik Hedling, "The Welfare State

Depicted," 182. On the national culture coding of Swedish cinematic landscape depiction in films from 1940 to 1959, see Per Olov Qvist, *Jorden är vår arvedel. Landsbygden i svensk spelfilm 1940–1959* (Uppsala: Filmhäftet, 1986).

26 The term comes from Jennifer M. Bean, "Post-Utopian European Cinema," *Aura: Film Studies Journal* 4, no. 3 (2000): 62–70; Erik Hedling's statement here is somewhat misleading. There are in fact very few shots of any distinctively urban character in the film; its suburban character, however, is emphasized. See Hedling, "The Welfare State Depicted," 191, 190.

27 Peter Cowie, *Ingmar Bergman: A Critical Biography* (New York: Charles Scribner's Sons, 1982), 197.

28 Cited in Erik Hedling, "The Welfare State Depicted," 187; Birgitta Steene with Eva Norin, *Måndagar med Bergman: En svensk publik möter Ingmar Bergmans filmer* (Stockholm: Brutus Östlings Bokförlag Symposion, 1996), 173. Hedling draws as well on Leif Zern, *Se Bergman* (Stockholm: Norstedts, 1993).

29 See also Erik Hedling, "Breaking the Swedish Sex Barrier."

30 Trevor Elkington's compelling analysis of the Nordic heritage film from the 1980s and 1990s includes a discussion of this genre's ties to literary adaptations and a thematic focus on coming-of-age stories. "Costumes, Adolescence, and Dogma: Nordic Film and American Distribution," in *Transnational Cinema in a Global North: Nordic Cinema in Transition*, ed. Andrew Nestingen and Trevor Elkington (Detroit, MI: Wayne State University Press, 2002), 31–54. On the European heritage film, see also Andrew Higson, "Re-presenting the National Past: Nostalgia and Pastiche in the Heritage Film," in *Fires Were Started: British Cinema and Thatcherism*, ed. Lester Friedman (Minneapolis: Minnesota University Press, 1993), 109–29.

31 Rosalind Galt, *The New European Cinema: Redrawing the Map* (New York: Columbia University Press, 2006), 7, 9.

32 See for example Josef Fares, *Jalla! Jalla!* (2000) and *Kopps!* (2003);

Ulf Malmros' *Slim Susie* (*Smala Sussie*, 2003); Kjell Sundvall's *The Guy in the Grave Next Door* (*Grabben i graven brevid*, 2002); Lars von Trier's *Dancer in the Dark* (2000); Daniel Lind Lagerlöf's *His and Hers* (*Hans och Hennes*, 2001); Maria Blom's *Dalecarlians* (*Masjävlar*, 2004); and Reza Bagher's *Popular Music from Vittula* (*Populärmusic från Vittula*, 2004).

33 See Ann-Kristin Wallengren, "Kultur och Okultur—Bilden Av Landsbygdens Folk," in *Solskenslandet: Svensk Film på 2000-Talet*, ed. Erik Hedling and Ann-Kristin Wallengren (Malmö: Atlantis, 2006).

34 For related arguments, see Andrew K. Nestingen, *Crime and Fantasy in Scandinavia: Fiction, Film, and Social Change* (Seattle: University of Washington Press, 2008), 7–8; Anna Westerståhl Stenport and Cecilia Alm, "Corporations, Crime, and Gender Construction in Stieg Larsson's *The Girl with the Dragon Tattoo*: Exploring Twenty-First Century Neoliberalism in Swedish Culture," *Scandinavian Studies* 81, no. 2 (2009): 157–78.

35 Von Trier's more recent films coproduced by Film i Väst and shot in Trollhättan, *Dogville* (Lions Gate Films, 2003) and *Manderlay* (IFC Films, 2005), mark an alternate trajectory in their extreme delocalization strategies. Substituting location shooting for abstract studio construction of an imagined space—a 1930s small town in Colorado (*Dogville*) and a southern US plantation (*Manderlay*)—these films anonymize the production location even further. Von Trier has often been featured in promotional material for the regionalization of the Swedish film industry and the film production center Film i Väst, yet two of his films shot there feature absolutely no recognizable representation of the region.

36 See also the report commissioned by Film i Väst, *Film Factory: Film i Väst 1992–2002*, ed. and text Marit Kapla (Trollhättan: Film i Väst, 2002), 6–15.

37 Toby Miller, *Global Hollywood 2* (London: BFI, 2005), 141. For a discussion of runaway production more generally, see ibid., 7; see also

Olof Hedling, "'Sveriges Mest Kända Korvkiosk': Om regionaliseringen av svensk film," in *Solskenslandet: Svensk Film på 2000-Talet*, ed. Erik Hedling and Ann-Kristin Wallengren (Malmö: Atlantis, 2006), 29–31.

38 Coproduction funding means any funding awarded to a film not stemming from the lead production company itself. See for example Per Neumann and Charlotte Appelgren, *The Fine Art of Coproducing*, 2nd ed. (Copenhagen: Neumann Publishing, 2007).

39 Anne Jäckel, *European Film Industries* (London: BFI, 2003), 24. For a general discussion of some of these changes, see also Mary P. Wood, *Contemporary European Cinema* (London: Hodder Arnold, 2007), 6–20.

40 Anders Annikas, *Fucking Vittula: en bok som nästan alla har läst, en film som nästan alla har sett, två städer där nästan ingen har varit* (Malmö: Doob, 2007), 79–81; Lukas Moodysson, research interview.

41 Some include "'alltid något' sa Fan när han kom till Åmål" (Well it is something, said the Devil when he came to Åmål); "Jag kom till Åmål, men det var stängt" (I got to Åmål, but it was closed); and "'En skam för mig men en ära för stan,' sa han som gick vilse i Åmål" (Shameful for me, but an honor to the town, said he who got lost in Åmål), as retold by Anders Annikas, *Fucking Vittula*, 118.

42 See Annikas, *Fucking Vittula*, 105.

43 Moodysson, research interview.

44 Ibid.

45 Ibid.

46 Ibid.

47 Ulf Brantås, Alexandra Dahlström, and Josefin Åsberg, research interviews.

48 Allan Pred, *Even in Sweden: Racisms, Racialized Spaces, and the Popular Geographical Imagination* (Berkeley: University of California Press, 2000).

49 Ibid., 215; see also the official SFI publication *Regionerna i centrum* (Stockholm: Svenska Filminstitutet, 2001), 28–29.

50 United Nations, Committee on the Elimination of Racial Discrimination. *Twelfth periodic reports of States parties due in 1995. Addendum. Sweden,* October 25, 1996, 3. Sweden had a total population of 8.8 million at the end of 1995 with 936,000 born abroad.

51 See for example Thomas Hammar, "Closing the Door to the Swedish Welfare State," in *Mechanisms of Immigration Control: A Comparative Analysis of European Regulation Policies,* ed. Grete Brochmann and Thomas Hammar (Oxford, UK: Berg, 1999), 169–201.

52 Film i Väst and the regionalization of the Swedish film industry have been the subject of a number of studies, as outlined below. In the following, I draw on these studies as well as on research interviews with Tomas Eskilsson, Katatrina Krave, Louise Martin, Lars Jönsson, Charlotte Appelqvist, and Jannike Åhlund. See Olof Hedling, "'Sveriges Mest Kända Korvkiosk,'" 19–50, and "A New Deal in European Film? Notes on the Swedish Regional Production Turn," *Film International* 35 (2007): 8–17; *Regionerna i centrum*; Margareta Dahlström, "Att Analysera Kopplingarna Mella Filmproduktion Och Regional Utveckling," in *Film Och Regional Utveckling i Norden,* ed. Margareta Dahlström (Stockholm: Svenska Filminstitutet, 2005), 13–37; Margareta Dahlström, "Regionaliserad Filmpolitik i Sverige," in *Film Och Regional Utveckling i Norden,* ed. Margareta Dahlström (Stockholm: Svenska Filminstitutet, 2005), 38–81; Roger Blomgren, *Den Onda, Den Goda Och Den Nyttiga—Kulturindustrin, Filmen Och Regionerna* (Trollhättan, Sweden: Högskolan Väst, 2007), 51–96; Roger Blomgren and Anna-Maria Blomgren, *Den svenska filmpolitikens regionalisering, eller varför går det så bra för Film i väst?* Unpublished report. Högskolan i Trollhättan/Uddevalla. Institutionen för arbete, ekonomi och hälsa. [2004?]; Per Assmo, "Creative Clusters—Ideas and Realities for Cluster Growth: The Example of Film in Väst in the Region of Västra Götaland, Sweden," in *Industrial Clusters and Inter-Firm Networks,* ed. Charlie Karlsson, Börje Johansson, and Rover R. Stough (Cheltenham, UK:

Edward Elgar, 2005), 453–74; Per Assmo, "Creative Industry Cluster Growth in a Global Economy: The Example of Film in Väst, Sweden," not published, University of Trollhättan/Uddevalla, Department of Economics and Informatics, 2004; Per Assmo and Roger Blomgren, *Film Production as Strategy for Regional Development—Mission (Im)Possible?* HTU Research Reports #3, no. 1. (Kungälv: Grafikerna AB, 2003); Solveig Arle, "Film i Väst," *Filmjournalen* (2001): 22–25; Film i Väst commissioned publications Film i Väst, *Filmfabriken: Film i väst 1992–2002*, ed. and text Marit Kapla (Trollhättan: Film i Väst, 2002) and *Film Factory: Film i Väst 1992–2002*, ed. and text Marit Kapla (Trollhättan: Film i Väst, 2002); *Film, TV och moderna medier i Västra Götaland*, ed. and text Per Stern, Martin Svensson, and Bengt Toll (Film i Väst, 2003).

53 The county of Älvsborg was one of the first regional entities in 1987 to include film production as an aspect of its cultural policy program. In 1990 the town of Alingsås became a local resource center in that county. The town of Trollhättan became the dominant site for film production in the region as Film i Väst (initially called Västernfilm) opened its offices in a former industrial area called Nohab in 1996.

54 Moodysson in Mats Weman, "Lukas Moodysson" [interview], in *Regionerna i centrum* (Stockholm: Svenska Filminstitutet, 2001), 26.

55 Lukas Moodysson, research interview.

56 Moodysson in Mats Weman, "Lukas Moodysson," 26–27; Moodysson, research interview.

57 See Olof Hedling, "'Sveriges Mest Kända Korvkiosk,'" 42–44.

58 Micheal Keating, "Europeanism and Regionalism," in *The European Union and the Regions*, ed. Barry J. Jones and Michael Keating (New York: Clarendon Press, 1995), 1.

59 European Commission, *The European Agenda for Culture*, 2007, http://ec.europa.eu/culture/our-policy-development/doc399_en.htm (accessed April 12, 2010); see also Katharine Sarikakis, *Media and Cultural Policy in the European Union* (Amsterdam: Rodopi, 2007).

60 Eskilsson, research interview.
61 Moodysson, research interview; see also interview in *Regionerna i centrum*. According to sources, SFI first rejected *Show Me Love* for production funding. After the film received coproduction funding from Film i Väst and the Danish Film Institute, SFI provided supplementary funding. Lars Jönsson and Tomas Eskilsson, research interviews.
62 Cf. Roger Blomgren, *Den Onda*, 56–62.
63 See Per Assmo, "Creative Clusters—Ideas and Realities for Cluster Growth," 453–74; Assmo, "Creative Industry Cluster Growth in a Global Economy;" Assmo and Blomgren, *Film Production as Strategy for Regional Development*; and Film i Väst, *Film, TV och moderna medier i Västra Götaland*.
64 Charlotte Appelqvist, research interview.
65 Katarina Krave, research interview.
66 In 1998, FiV had revenue of approximately 31 million SEK and awarded 14 million SEK in direct production support; in 2004 revenue was 63 million and production support awarded was 44 million. In 2009, revenue was 94 million. Ibid.
67 Cineregio, www.cineregio.org (accessed April 15, 2007).
68 Film i Vast, *Filmfabriken*, 22–23.
69 Eskilsson, research interview; Blomgren, *Den Onda*, 63–66.
70 Tomas Eskilsson, "Att leda regionala utvecklingsprocesser," in *Att Mobilisera för regional tillväxt. Regionala utvecklingsprocesser, kluster och innovationssystem*, ed. Lars Christensen and Peter Kempinsky (Lund: Studentlitteratur, 2004), 91; other sources mention higher numbers.
71 Thomas Elsaesser, *European Cinema: Face to Face with Hollywood* (Amsterdam: Amsterdam University Press, 2005); Galt, *The New European Cinema*; Jäckel, *European Film Industries*; Rivi, *European Cinema After 1989*; and Wood, *Contemporary European Cinema*.

72 Bengt Toll, research interview; see also Cineregio, www.cineregio.org (accessed April 15, 2007).
73 Quotations from Blomgren and Blomgren, cited in Olof Hedling "'Sveriges Mest Kända Korvkiosk,'" 24.
74 Ibid.
75 Jill Forbes and Sarah Street, *European Cinema: An Introduction* (London: Palgrave, 2001), 27. Many other scholars argue this as well; see for example Wood, *Contemporary European Cinema*, 24–48.
76 Galt, *The New European Cinema*, 3. See also Mark Betz, "The Name above the (Sub)title: Internationalism, Coproductions, and Polyglot European Cinema," *Camera Obscura* 46, no. 6 (2001): 1–44; Tim Bergfelder, "The Nation Vanishes: European Co-Productions and Popular Genre Formula in the 1950s and 1960s," in *Cinema and Nation*, ed. Mette Hjort and Scott Mackenzie (London: Routledge, 2000), 131–42.
77 Mette Hjort, "From Epiphanic Culture to Circulation: The Dynamics of Globalization in Nordic Cinema," in *Transnational Cinema in a Global North: Nordic Cinema in Transition*, ed. Trevor Elkington and Andrew Nestingen (Detroit, MI: Wayne State University Press, 2005), 191.
78 Elsaesser, *European Cinema*, 15.
79 Eva af Geijerstam, "After Bergman: New Directions in Swedish Film," in *Film in Sweden*, ed. Francesco Bono and Maaret Koskinen (Stockholm: The Swedish Institute, 1996), 57.
80 The Swedish Film Institute awarded significant funding to several international coproductions from 1966 to 1986, including Robert Bresson's *Au hazard Balthazar* (1966), Henning Carlsen's *Sult* (1966), Susan Sontag's *Brother Carl* (1972), José Luis Borau's *Sabina* (1979), Michael Raeburn's *The Grass is Singing / Killing Heat* (1981), Hrafn Gunnlaugsson's *When the Raven Flies* (1984), Andrei Tarkovsky's *The Sacrifice* (1986).
81 Tytti Soila, Astrid Söderbergh Widding, and Gunnar Iversen argue

in the introduction to *Nordic National Cinemas* that the concept of national cinema is made concrete generally at the reception and audience level but that "Nordic cinema has been national in the specific sense that it has not, or to only a limited extent, been exportable to other countries." "Introduction: Film Production as a National Project," in *Nordic National Cinemas*, ed. Tytti Soila, Astrid Söderbergh Widding, and Gunnar Iversen (London: Routledge, 1998), 2. Nestingen and Elkington, drawing partly on Toby Miller's concept of *Global Hollywood*, argue that "thinking of the films of the Nordic countries as national texts . . . is inaccurate and misleading when trying to understand the elements of any given film in times of globalization and cultural transition." Trevor Elkington and Andrew Nestingen, "Introduction. Transnational Nordic Cinema," in *Transnational Cinema in a Global North: Nordic Cinema in Transition*, ed. Andrew Nestingen and Trevor Elkington (Detroit, MI: Wayne State University Press, 2002), 1–28; Toby Miller, *Global Hollywood* (London: BFI, 2001).

82 Wallengren, "Kultur och Okultur," 51.

83 Blomgren, *Den Onda,* 5; see also Per Olov Qvist and Tytti Soila, "Eva den ustötta/Swedish and underage," in *The Cinema of Scandinavia*, ed. Tytti Soila (London: Wallflower, 2005), 151.

84 On the Swedish Film Institute's role and function for film production in Sweden, see Mikael Timm, *Dröm och förbannad verklighet: Spelet om svensk film under 40 år* (Stockholm: Svenska Filminstitutet, 2003); see also Blomgren, *Den Onda,* 38–50. During the 1970s and 1980s, SFI produced films, including SFI director Jörn Donner, credited as producer of Ingmar Bergman's *Fanny and Alexander* [*Fanny och Alexander*] (Svensk filmindustri, 1982).

85 Pil Gundelach Brandstrup and Eva Novrup Redvall, "Breaking the Borders: Danish Coproductions in the 1990s," in *Transnational Cinema in a Global North: Nordic Cinema in Transition*, ed. Andrew Nestingen and Trevor Elkington (Detroit, MI: Wayne State University

Press, 2002), 147; see also Hjort, "From Epiphanic Culture to Circulation," 197–98.

86 Brandstrup and Redvall, "Breaking the Borders," 147.
87 See for example Brandstrup and Redvall, "Breaking the Borders,"147–48; Hjort, "From Epiphanic Culture to Circulation," 191.
88 Elkington and Nestingen, "Introduction. Transnational Nordic Cinema," 2–4. German is a fourth national language used in the film, as well.
89 Ibid., 5.
90 Timm, *Dröm och förbannad verklighet*,142; see also Per Andersson, "Memfis, Stockholm," *Teknik och Människa* (June 2005): 8–9.
91 Lars Jönsson, research interview.
92 See for example Roger Wilson, "Sista Föreställningen," *Fokus* 35 (2006): 24–33; see also Stig Björkman, Helena Lindblad, and Fredrik Sahlin, *Fucking Film: Den Nya Svenska Filmen* (Stockholm: Alfabeta Anamma, 2002).
93 See also Annika Lindskog, "Sweden in the Eye of the Beholder: Colin Nutley's House of Angels and Swedish Identity," *Scandinavica: An International Journal of Scandinavian Studies* 44, no. 2 (2005): 162–82.
94 Sveriges Television Drama, as led by Gunnar Carlsson, a former director of Gothenburg International Film Festival, has been particularly significant for this development; few feature films are made in Sweden today without SvT coproduction funding.
95 International and EU contexts have also been significant for Memfis' evolution as a production company. Jönsson explains in a research interview, "In the mid-1990s, I attended international courses and benefited from networking opportunities organized by the EU *MEDIA* program; these gave opportunities for meeting with a range of European producers and other film industry professionals, which allowed me to build a network to draw upon for coproductions. These also taught me how to navigate within big international coproduc-

tion like *Breaking the Waves* [October Films, 1996] and to find good collaborators across Europe." Jönssson was executive producer for the main production company Zentropa on *Breaking the Waves*.
96 See also Nestingen, *Crime and Fantasy in Scandinavia*, 76–77.
97 Cf. Philip Martin, *Sidetracked; Firewall; One Step Behind*, BBC, PBS, TV-series, 2008.

4. MOODYSSON'S CONTINUATION

1 Lukas Moodysson, *Mammoth* [*Mammut*] (Memfis DVD, 2009); *Together* [*Tillsammans*] (Memfis DVD, 2000).
2 The film was well received across the board in the Swedish media and sold about 883,000 tickets in Sweden (population less than 9 million). *Svensk filmdatabas*, Svenska Filminstitutet, http://www.sfi.se/en-gb/Swedish-film-database/ (accessed April 12, 2010). It screened out of competition to great acclaim at the 2000 Venice Film Festival and Toronto Film Festival. *Together* did not receive any *Guldbagge* awards (the Swedish Oscar equivalent), but it won multiple international awards. These include the New Directors Showcase Award at the Seattle International Film Festival, 2001, the Taos Land Grant Award at the Taos, New Mexico, Film Festival; in Europe, the Bratislava International Film Festival, the International Film Festival in Ghent, Belgium in 2000 and the special jury prize at the Festival du Film in Paris in 2001. Other French prizes were awarded at the Mamer Film Festival and the Festival of Comedy Film sin Alpe d'Huez. Moodysson was also nominated for the European Discovery 2000 Fassbinder Award.
3 The film premiered at 14 London cinemas in July 2001 and was distributed in 45 copies for its 2001 release in the United States. These are unusually large numbers for subtitled foreign films in their respective markets. *Together* was greeted enthusiastically in both the United Kingdom and the United States. An unnamed US company bought the

rights to a remake in 2002, and these rights have been renewed. Lars Jönsson, research interview.

4 See Magnus Sundholm, "*Tillsammans* tredje bästa film i USA," *Arbetet*, December 15, 2001. For best-film lists, see the production notes to the Swedish DVD version of Lukas Moodysson, *Lilya 4-ever* [*Lilja 4-ever*] (Memfis DVD, 2002).

5 A parallel can be made to Carl Theodor Dreyer, who was famously fetishistic about immersing actors in unusually functional film sets with authentic props, decor, etc. In *Master of the House* [*Du skal ære din hustru*] (Palladium Film, 1925), he insisted that a complete apartment be built in the studio, with four walls, running water, and electric lights. While invisible to the camera, the authenticity of the environment would permeate the actors' performances. These kinds of cinematic experiments also reflect a long-standing investment in naturalism by Scandinavian theater and film directors.

6 Carl Johan de Geer, "Om en märklig inspelning," *Aftonbladet*, August 27, 2000.

7 For particularly insightful analyses that take gendered aspects into account, see Yvonne Hirdman, "Social Engineering and the Woman Question: Sweden in the 1930s," in *Swedish Social Democracy: A Model in Transition*, ed. Wallace Clement and Rianne Mahon (Toronto: Canadian Scholars' Press, 1994), 65–79; Yvonne Hirdman, "The Social Engineers, the Rationalist Utopia, and the New Home of the 1930s," *International Journal of Political Economy* 22, no. 2 (1992): 27–49.

8 As Ursula Lindqvist argues, "Swedish-style social democracy is deeply nationalist in orientation, yet its anchoring in the symbolic site of the home imbues it with a nurturing, non-aggressive nature." "The Cultural Archive of the IKEA Store," *Space and Culture* 12, no. 1 (2009): 45.

9 Such statements are reflected in numerous Swedish and international publications published in conjunction with domestic and interna-

tional releases of *Together*, *Lilya 4-ever*, *The New Country* [*Det nya landet*], a four-part television series (SvT) and screenplay by Lukas Moodysson and Peter Birro, Göta Film, 2000. See for example Mats Weman, "Pastor Moodyssons Bekännelser," *Nöjesguiden*, September 9, 2000; Mattias Göransson, "Efter Fucking Åmål," *DN Lördag Söndag*, August 19, 2000; Karen Durbin, "When Love Thought It Could Defeat War," *The New York Times*, August 19, 2001.

10 Kevin Conroy Scott, "Lukas Moodysson: *Together*," in *Screenwriters' Masterclass: Screenwriters Talk About Their Greatest Movies*, ed. Kevin Conroy Scott (London: Faber and Faber, 2005), 260–61.

11 *The New Country* was released as a feature film later that year. Lukas Moodysson and Stefan Jarl, *The Kids They Sentenced* [*Terrorister: En film om dom dömda*] (Folkets Bio, 2003). Stefan Jarl is one of Sweden's best-known documentary filmmakers.

12 Tigervall provides a very insightful reading of the genre characteristics and the characterization. Cecilia Tigervall, "Folkhemsk film med 'invandraren' i rollen som den sympatiske Andre" (PhD diss., Umeå University, 2005), 101–12.

13 This is more than one-fifth of Sweden's adult population. Göransson, "Efter Fucking Åmål."

14 *The New Country*, http://en.wikipedia.org/wiki/The_New_Country (accessed April 12, 2010).

15 Rochelle Wright, "'Immigrant Film' in Sweden at the Millenium," in *Transnational Cinema in a Global North: Nordic Cinema in Transition*, ed. Trevor Elkington and Andrew Nestingen (Detroit, MI: Wayne State University Press, 2005), 62; see also Amanda Doxtater, "Bodies in Elevators: The Conveyance of Ethnicity in Recent Swedish Films," in *Northern Constellations: New Readings in Nordic Cinema*, ed. C. Claire Thomas (Norwich, UK: Norvik Press, 2006), 59–77. These films include Josef Fares, *Jalla! Jalla!* (Memfis, 2000); Reza Bagher, *Wings of Glass* [*Vingar av glas*] (Chimney Pot, 2000); Reza Parza, *Before the Storm* [*Före stormen*] (Göteborg: Västra

Götlands län, 2000); Susan Taslimi, *All Hell Let Loose* [*Hus i helvete*] (Film i Väst, 2002); and Josef Fares, *Zozo* (Memfis, 2005). *The New Country* also reflects an increased contemporary public debate about segregation and ethnic prejudice in Swedish society, as well as the notion of a "Fortress Europe" with restrictive immigration and asylum-granting policies. See Tigervall, "Folkhemsk film," 98–100.

16 Cyrill Hellman, *Stefan Jarl: En intervjubok* (Stockholm: Kartago, 2008), 280, 285; Nicholas Wennö, "Radikal filmarduo låter aktivisterna tala ut," *Dagens Nyheter*, June 18, 2003. Like similar protests in Seattle in 1999 against the World Trade Organization or in Genoa in 2001 against the Group of Eight Summit, participants in what has been called *Göteborgskravallerna* rallied in protest of American imperialism and neoliberal capitalism. The responses included, in a Swedish context, relatively harsh sentencing for young adults and teenagers. Moodysson expresses: "I wanted to hear authentic voices" (Hellman 285). Jarl concedes, "They [those sentenced] had not been heard in media. We wanted to give them a voice. The press and prosecutors had already sentenced them. We wanted to listen to the kids themselves" (Hellman 280).

Ingrid Esping's thorough and insightful article gives background and detailed analysis of the film's reception in Sweden, including a number of sources that outline the social and political reactions to the demonstrations. Ingrid Esping, "Terrorister—en film om dom dömda: Subjektiva upplevelser av våld och orätt efter Göteborgskravallerna," in *Solskenslandet: Svensk film på 2000-talet* (Malmö: Atlantis, 2006), 221–44. See also Mikael Löfgren and Masoud Vatankhah, eds., *Vad hände med Sverige i Göteborg?* (Stockholm: Ordfront, 2002); Mikael Oskarson, "Lag eller ordning? Polisens hantering av EU-toppmötet i Göteborg 2001" (PhD diss., Stockholms universitet, 2005).

17 Esping, "Terrorister," 222.
18 The film premiered on only a handful of Swedish screens in the middle

of summer, traditionally the yearly low point in Swedish cinema admission numbers. Yet over 145 news media articles were published about the film in its first week of cinema release, and it received a total box office tally of 15,870 tickets, a respectable number in comparison with other documentaries screened in cinemas in 2003 (Esping, "Terrorister," 222). Jarl claims over 20,000 tickets were sold. Hellman, *Stefan Jarl*, 282. In addition, *The Kids They Sentenced* "was one of *Folkets Bio*'s most commonly rented films to schools, organizations, and seminars during 2003," which significantly increased unofficial audience numbers; it has also been distributed for personal viewing in DVD form and on the internet (Esping 222). The film had invitations to screen at over twenty international film festivals and was under consideration for international release, but its distribution was thwarted by the fact that one of the participants refused in the final stages of production to authorize his participation in the film for such wide release and consented to inclusion only if his face would be blurred, according to Jarl (Hellman, *Stefan Jarl*, 283). As Esping phrases it, *The Kids They Sentenced* became "sentenced to silence" by the unintended limited distribution (222).

19 The name of the historical young woman is Danguole Rasalaite, born in Lithuania in 1983. Abandoned by her mother at age 16, she had been lured by her boyfriend to Sweden. Forced to engage in prostitution, she had been held captive in an apartment in Arlöv, just outside Malmö (near Moodysson's home) since November 1999. She committed suicide by jumping to her death from a highway overpass on January 7, 2000. See biographical paragraph, untitled, in Ola Florin et al., eds., *Vad har mitt liv med Lilja att göra?* (Stockholm: Svenska Filminstitutet, 2004), 7.

20 Lukas Moodysson, "Jag gör filmer för att väcka människor som sover," in *Vad har mitt liv med Lilja att göra?*, 13–14. See also Moodysson's acceptance speech for the Swedish *Guldbagge* Awards in 2003. Lukas Moodysson, "Detta är den värld vi lever i," in *Vad har*

mitt liv med Lilja att göra?, 91. It is clear that the film struck a chord among viewers, including those with personal and professional experience of trafficking. "Everyone—from someone at an orphanage in Chile and the Swedish foreign minister—got in touch." After showing the film to "25–30 people from Eastern Europe, mainly women, who are working with trafficking and prostitution in their countries, I was quite happy to hear that they thought the film was accurate." Danny Leigh, "Lukas Moodysson at the NFT," *The Guardian* (London), November 20, 2002. This interview is also available as an extra on the UK-released DVD of *Lilja 4-ever*.

21 Leigh, "Lukas Moodysson at the NFT." Cf. Scott, "Lukas Moodysson: *Together*," 254; David Noh, "Hardcore Spiritualism: Sweden's Lukas Moodysson Explores Personal Vision in *Lilja 4-Ever*," *Film Journal International* 106, no. 5 (2003): 18–20.

22 Moodysson suggests that Lilya's friend Volodya (Artyom Bogucharsky) "became a metaphor for Jesus [...]. I like the idea of Jesus as a little boy who is very kind and tries to do everything he can to save this girl." See Leigh, "Lukas Moodysson at the NFT."

23 Olof Hedling outlines the complexity in the Swedish establishment's response to the film in "Om 'Lilja 4-Ever'—En Svensk Film," in *Från Eden Till Damavdelningen: Studier Om Kvinnan i Litteraturen: En Vänbok Till Christina Sjöblad*, ed. Bibi Jonsson, Karin Nykvist, and Birthe Sjöberg (Absalon: Skrifter utgivna vid Litteraturvetenskapliga institutionen i Lund, 2004), 323–34.

24 As Carolina Wennerholm notes, this law is unusually radical in a European context and was hotly debated. Carolina Johansson Wennerholm, "Crossing Borders and Bridges: The Baltic Region Networking Project," *Gender and Development* 10, no. 1 (2002): 10–19; see also Yvonne Svanström, "En självklar efterfrågan," in *Vad har mitt liv med Lilja att göra?*, 45–57.

25 The film was distributed as mandatory viewing in all Swedish high schools and to those pursuing the military service. See Anna Sparr-

man, "Film as a Political and Educational Device: Talk about Men, Male Sexuality and Gender among Swedish Youth," *Visual Studies* 21, no. 2 (2006): 167–82; Daniel Lundquist and Klas Viklund, *"Lilja 4-Ever" på Skolbi: Dokumentation Av Svenska Filminstitutets Insatser Kring "Lilja 4-Ever" på Skolbio i Sverige 2003–2004* (Stockholm: Svenska Filminstitutet: 2005). On international distribution, see Hedling, "Om *"Lilja 4-Ever"*—En Svensk Film," 327; Lars Kristensen, "Divergent Accounts of Equivalent Narratives: Russian-Swedish *Interdevochka* Meets Swedish-Russian *Lilya 4-ever*," *Portal: Journal of Multidisciplinary International Studies* 4, no. 2 (2007): 1–5.

26 The *Guldbagge* awards were for best directing and best screenplay (Moodysson), best film (Jönsson), best cinematography (Ulf Brantås), and best actor (Oksana Akinshina). The film won the Nordic Audience Award at Gothenburg International Film Festival and a number of international awards, including film festivals in Gijon, Limassol, Harare, Rouen, and Brasilia. Over 325,000 tickets were sold at the Swedish box office, which is a respectable number for a Swedish film but significantly less than previous Moodysson feature films.

27 Rayns' review in *Sight and Sound* is very critical, however. Tony Rayns, *"Lilya 4-ever,"* film review, *Sight and Sound* 13, no. 5 (2003): 56–58; see also Obf Hedling, "Om *Lilja 4-Ever*—En Svensk Film," 327–28; and Kristensen, "Divergent Accounts of Equivalent Narratives," 6–7, 15. A number of interviews with Moodysson were published in international publications upon the release of this film, as it was an eagerly anticipated follow-up to *Together*. In these interviews international journalists appear intrigued by this filmmaker's subject choices, including his focus on young women.

28 Lars Von Trier, *Breaking the Waves* (October Films, 1996). One of the films in the Golden Heart Trilogy, it also features a young woman character as an innocent prostitute.

29 See Kristensen, "Divergent Accounts of Equivalent Narratives,"

18–20; Andrew K. Nestingen, *Crime and Fantasy in Scandinavia: Fiction, Film, and Social Change* (Seattle: University of Washington Press, 2008), 130.

30 Fran Markowitz, *Coming of Age in Post-Soviet Russia* (Urbana: University of Illinois Press, 2000), 189.

31 Mark Steinberg and Catherine Wanner, "Introduction: Reclaiming the Sacred After Communism," in *Religion, Morality, and Community in post-Soviet Aesthetics*, ed. Mark D. Steinberg and Catherine Wanner (Washington, DC: Woodrow Wilson Center Press; 2008), 1.

32 Markowitz, *Coming of Age in Post-Soviet Russia* (2000), 132–34.

33 Lukas Moodysson and Jesper Kurlandsky, research interviews.

34 *A Hole in My Heart* [*Ett Hål i Mitt Hjärta*] (Memfis DVD, 2005).

35 Like all other Moodysson films, *A Hole in My Heart* was produced by Lars Jönsson at Memfis. It was coproduced by Film i Väst, Zentropa, Sveriges Television, and Canal + Stockholm. Additional funding support came from SFI, the Nordic Film and TV Fund, DFI, and the EU Media Programme. Reviews in the Swedish press had some praise, while critics in the United States and the United Kingdom were overwhelmingly negative. Manohla Dargis, "Pornographers at Work in a Circular World," *The New York Times*, April 8, 2005; Ryan Gilbey, "A Hole in My Heart," *Sight and Sound*, February 2005, http://www.bfi.org.uk/sightandsound/review/589/ (accessed April 12, 2010); J. Hoberman, "A Squalid Swedish Porno Drama Punishes Its Audience," *The Village Voice*, March 29, 2005; Anthony Lane, "Feelings," *New Yorker*, April 11, 2005, 86–87; James Mottram, "A Hole in My Heart," *Film Review* 653 (2005): 104. Though nominated for a European film award, it was not well received by the public. Only a little over 25,000 tickets were sold in Sweden. *Svensk filmdatabas* (accessed April 12, 2010). For a critical introduction to the film, see Mariah Larsson, "Om Kön, Sexualitet Och Moral i *Ett Hål i Mitt Hjärta*," in *Solskenslandet: Svensk Film på 2000-Talet* (Malmö: Atlantis, 2006), 245–67.

36 Lukas Moodysson, research interview.
37 The crew consisted of Moodysson, Jesper Kurlandsky, Malin Fornander, Kalle Strandlind, and, for final editing, Michal Leszczylowski. Moodysson also emphasizes the collaborative process of the script, which indicates a break with Moodysson's tightly constructed screenplays. All crew and actors are included as cowriters in the credits. Leszczylowski affirms in a research interview that editing this film was one of the most demanding and difficult projects he has ever undertaken. He had extensive material to work with and a subject matter he found difficult. Many of the scenes were "uncomfortably graphic, very explicit" and "they affected me deeply." Michal Leszczylowski, research interview.
38 This film involved a break with two longtime collaborators: director of photography Ulf Brantås and B photographer Trolle Davidson.
39 A B photographer is an assistant cameraman, sometimes called a focus puller; Moodysson refers in this quote to the fact that the B photographer often adjusts focus during a shot; he is physically shaping the image with his hand.
40 Moodysson, research interview.
41 Ibid.
42 Moodysson and Kurlandsky, research interviews.
43 Lukas Moodysson, *Container* (Umeå: Atrium, 2009). The art installation *Containermuseum* showed at the renowned Stockholm gallery Färgfabriken in March 2006; http://www.fargfabriken.se/index.php?tabell=content&id=78&imgnr=3 (accessed April 12, 2010). A modified version was shown at the Institute of Contemporary Art in London in October 2006, then called *Inside the Head of Lukas Moodysson: The Container Crypt*, art exhibit, London: Institute of Contemporary Art, http://www.ica.org.uk/Inside%20the%20Head%20of%20Lukas%20Moodysson%3A%20The %20Container%20Crypt+12073.twl (accessed April 12, 2010).
44 Slightly fewer than 800 tickets were sold in Sweden. *Svensk filmda-*

tabas (accessed April 12, 2010). Swedish reviews were very mixed. Some, like the conservative newspaper *Svenska Dagbladet*, gave it six out of six points and lauded it as Sweden's second best film of 2006, while other outlets indicated admiration mixed with apprehension toward Moodysson's continued work in the experimental, narrow, and arguably obscure. "Årets bästa filmer," *Svenska Dagbladet*, December 29, 2006. *Container* was reviewed less than positively in the British Film Institute's journal *Sight and Sound*; see Gilbey, "A Hole in My Heart."

45 Moodysson, *Mammoth*.
46 Coproducers include Zentropa Denmark and Zentropa Germany, Film i Väst, and Sveriges Television; additional funding came from the Swedish Film Institute, Danish Film Institute, *Eurimages*, Filmförderungsanstalt Berlin (FFA), European Union Media Programme, Nordic Film and Television Fund (NFTF), and Medienboard Berlin Brandenburg (MBBB). This extensive support list shows the skill of both Memfis and Zentropa at gaining coproduction and other funding allocations. It also illustrates Moodysson's status at the time as a major filmmaker. In Sweden, *Mammoth* claimed the top spot in ticket sales its first week and was generally received with respect by critics in major Swedish news outlets. Malena Janson writes in *Svenska Dagbladet*, however, that "Moodysson can do better than this" and gives the film three points out of six possible. Malena Janson, "Moodysson kan bättre," *Svenska Dagbladet*, January 22, 2009.

Mammoth was screened at a number of international film festivals in 2009, including in Vancouver, Chicago, the Hamptons, Bangkok, Sarajevo, Sao Paolo, and Rio de Janeiro (more are listed on http://www.imdb.com/title/tt1038043/releaseinfo#akas). But it garnered few prizes and limited recognition. The film has been distributed for cinema release in the Nordic countries, the United States by IFC films, the United Kingdom, the Netherlands, and the Czech Republic.

47 *Svensk filmdatabas* (accessed April 12, 2010).

48 Several reviewers remark that at the press screening in Berlin, booing outweighed applause. Reviews by international critics in print press and online were largely negative. See for example "*Mammoth* movie review," *The New York Times*, November 20, 2009; James Walling, "The Poetry of Pain," *The Prague Post*, March 17, 2010; Erik Jensen, "Moralen helt i halsen," *Politiken* (Copenhagen), February 10, 2009; Nick James, "Berlin Film Festival," *The Observer* (London), February 15, 2009; Andy Lauer, "Cinemadaily: '*Mammoth*' Letdown," *Indiewire*, November 20, 2009, http://www.indiewire.com/article/cinemadaily_mammoth_letdown/ (accessed April 12, 2010); Eric Hynes, "Review: Distant Voices, Shrill Lives: Lukas Moodysson's *Mammoth*," *Indiewire*, November 16, 2009, http://www.indiewire.com/article/review_distant_voices_shrill_lives_lukas_Moodyssons_mammoth/ (accessed April 12, 2010).

49 In the first two-thirds of the film, for example, cuts are made to replicate exactly the time difference between New York City and Thailand or the Philippines. Moodysson and Leszczylowski, research interviews. Cuts between the different story lines are tied together by overlap in thematic dialogue, as well as through music continuity. Leszczylowski's craftsmanship as a master film editor is clearly visible in this film.

50 Leszczylowski, research interview.

FESTIVAL SCREENINGS AND AWARDS

1 Data provided by Memfis film and supplemented by information provided by Svenska Filminstitutet. The list is ordered chronologically.
2 Data provided by Memfis film.

Bibliography

RESEARCH INTERVIEWS

Åhlund, Jannike. Göteborg, Sweden. January 30, 2008.
Appelqvist, Charlotte. Göteborg, Sweden. June 16, 2009.
Åsberg, Josefin. Göteborg, Sweden. June 6, 2009.
Assmo, Per. Trollhättan, Sweden. June 16, 2009.
Blomgren, Roger. Trollhättan, Sweden. June 15, 2009.
Brantås, Ulf. Stockholm, Sweden. June 10, 2009.
Dahlström, Alexandra. Stockholm, Sweden. June 10, 2009.
Denward, Charlotta. Göteborg, Sweden. August 5, 2009.
Eskilsson, Tomas. Göteborg, Sweden. January 29, 2009.
Gentele, Jeanette. Stockholm, Sweden. June 11, 2009.
Jönsson, Lars. Stockholm, Sweden. June 9, 2009.
Krave, Katarina. Trollhättan, Sweden. June 16, 2009.
Kurlandsky, Jesper. Stockholm, Sweden. June 10, 2009.
Leszczylowski, Michal. Stockholm, Sweden. June 10, 2009.
Martin, Louise. Göteborg, Sweden. January 30, 2008.
Moodysson, Lukas. Järnforsen, Småland, Sweden. July 24, 2009.
Timm, Mikael. Stockholm, Sweden. June 15, 2009.
Toll, Bengt. Stockholm, Sweden. June 15, 2009.

WORKS CITED

Aaron, Michele. "New Queer Cinema: An Introduction." In *New Queer Cinema: A Critical Reader*, edited by Michele Aaron, 3–14. Edinburgh: Edinburgh University Press, 2004.

Åhlund, Jannike. *New Cinema in Sweden*. Stockholm: Swedish Institute, 2002.

Ambjörnsson, Fanny. "Vem forskar om Agnes och Elin?" *Bang: Feministisk kulturtidskrift* 1 (1991): 33–38.

Andersson, Jan-Olov. "En fucking skit-bra film." *Aftonbladet*, October 23, 1998.

Andersson, Per. "Memfis, Stockholm." *Teknik och Människa* (June 2005): 8–9.

Annikas, Anders. *Fucking Vittula: en bok som nästan alla har läst, en film som nästan alla har sett, två städer där nästan ingen har varit*. Malmö: Doob, 2007.

Ansen, David. "Teen Spleen." *Newsweek*, October 18, 1999.

Applebaum, Stephen. "Swedehearts." *The New Scotsman*, February 26, 2000.

"Årets bästa filmer." *Svenska Dagbladet*, December 29, 2006. www.svd.se (accessed April 12, 2010).

Arle, Solveig. "Film i Väst." *Filmjournalen* (2001): 22–25.

Assmo, Per. "Creative Clusters—Ideas and Realities for Cluster Growth: The Example of Film in Väst in the Region of Västra Götaland, Sweden." In *Industrial Clusters and Inter-Firm Networks*, edited by Charlie Karlsson, Börje Johansson, and Rover R. Stough, 453–74. Cheltenham, UK: Edward Elgar, 2005.

———. "Creative Industry Cluster Growth in a Global Economy: The Example of Film in Väst, Sweden." Not published. University of Trollhättan/Uddevalla, Department of Economics and Informatics. 2004.

Assmo, Per, and Roger Blomgren. *Film Production as Strategy for Regional Development—Mission (Im)Possible?* HTU Research Report 3, no. 1. Kungälv: Grafikerna AB, 2003.

Bean, Jennifer M. "Post-Utopian European Cinema." *Aura: Film Studies Journal* 4, no. 3 (2000): 62–70.

Benshoff, Harry, and Sean Griffin. "General Introduction." In *Queer Cinema: The Film Reader*, edited by Harry Benshoff and Sean Griffin, 1–15. New York: Routledge, 2005.

Bergfelder, Tim. "The Nation Vanishes: European Co-Productions and Popular Genre Formula in the 1950s and 1960s." In *Cinema and Nation*, edited by Mette Hjort and Scott Mackenzie, 131–42. London: Routledge, 2000.

Bergman, Ingmar. *Bergmans 1900-Tal: En Hyllning Till Svensk Film, Från Victor Sjöström Till Lukas Moodysson*. Edited by Gunnar Bergdahl. Göteborg: Göteborg Film Festival, 2000.

Betz, Mark. "The Name above the (Sub)title: Internationalism, Coproductions, and Polyglot European Cinema." *Camera Obscura* 46, no. 6 (2001): 1–44.

Björklund, Jenny. "Queering the Small Town: Lukas Moodysson's Film *Show Me Love*." *Women's Studies* 39, no. 1 (2010): 37–51.

Björkman, Stig, Helena Lindblad, and Fredrik Sahlin. *Fucking Film: Den Nya Svenska Filmen*. Stockholm: Alfabeta Anamma, 2002.

Blomgren, Anna-Maria, and Roger Blomgren. *Den svenska filmpolitikens regionalisering, eller varför går det så bra för Film i Väst?* Högskolan i Trollhättan/Uddevalla. Institutionen för arbete, ekonomi och hälsa. http://www.hum.au.dk/ckulturf/pages/archive/activities/abstracts/papers/RogerBlomgren.pdf (accessed April 12, 2010).

Blomgren, Roger. *Den Onda, Den Goda Och Den Nyttiga—Kulturindustrin, Filmen Och Regionerna*. Trollhättan, Sweden: Högskolan Väst, 2007.

Brandstrup, Pil Gundelach, and Eva Novrup Redvall. "Breaking the Borders: Danish Coproductions in the 1990s." In *Transnational Cinema in a Global North: Nordic Cinema in Transition*, edited by Andrew Nestingen and Trevor Elkington, 141–63. Detroit, MI: Wayne State University Press, 2002.

Broder, Daniel. "Underground." Performed by Broder Daniel. Jimmy Fun Music/EMI Music, 1998.

Bronski, Michael. "Positive Images and the Coming Out Film." *Screen* 26, no. 1 (2000): 20–27.

Brooks, Xan. "Dirty Business." *The Guardian* (London), January 4, 2005.

Brownstein, Bill. "Show Me Love, not sex: A sensitively told Lesbian love story." *The Gazette* (Montreal), October 30, 1999.

Butler, Judith. *Bodies That Matter: On the Discursive Limits of "Sex."* London: Routledge, 1993.

———. *Gender Trouble: Feminism and the Subversion of Identity.* London: Routledge, 1990.

Byrnes, Paul. "Girl Meets Girl in Teen Romance with a Twist." *Morning Herald* (Sydney), December 14, 2000.

Cineregio. www.cineregio.org (accessed April 15, 2007).

Cowie, Peter. *Ingmar Bergman: A Critical Biography.* New York: Charles Scribner's Sons, 1982.

Cramby, Jonas. "Fucking Great." *Expressen* (Stockholm), October 23, 1998.

Croneman, Johan. "Längtan bort förlamar och frigör." *Dagens Nyheter*, October 23, 1998.

Dabelsteen, Per. "Interview: En Rejse Fra og til Helvedet." *Politiken* (Copenhagen), September 27, 2002.

Dahlquist, Marina. "Snow-White: The Aesthetic and Narrative Use of Snow in Swedish Silent Film." In *Nordic Explorations in Film Before 1930*, edited by John Fullerton and Jan Olsson, 226–48. Sydney, Australia: John Libbey, 1999.

Dahlström, Margareta. "Regionaliserad Filmpolitik i Sverige." In *Film och Regional Utveckling i Norden*, 38–81. Stockholm: Svenska Filminstitutet, 2005.

Dahlström, Margareta, Brita Hermelin, and Elisabeth Wengström. "Regionaliserad filmpolitik i Sverige." In *Film och regional utveckling i Norden*, 39–82. Stockholm: Svenska Filminstitutet, 2005.

Dahlström, Margareta, Brita Hermelin, and Grete Rusten. "Att analysera kopplingarna mellan filmproduktion och regional utveckling." In *Film och regional utveckling i Norden*, 13–37. Stockholm: Svenska Filminstitutet, 2005.

Dargis, Manohla. "Pornographers at Work in a Circular World." *The New York Times*, April 8, 2005.

———. "*Mammoth*. Movie review." *The New York Times*, November 20, 2009.

De Castella, Tom. "Revival—Tom de Castella charts how Swedish film finally cast off Bergman's shadow." *New Statesman*, September 15, 2003.

De Geer, Carl Johan. "Om en märklig inspelning." *Aftonbladet*, August 27, 2000.

De Lauretis, Teresa. "Queer Theory: Lesbian and Gay Studies: An Introduction." *Differences: A Journal of Feminist Cultural Studies* 3, no. 2 (1991): iii–xviii.

Dennis, Jeffrey P. *Queering Teen Culture: All-American Boys and Same Sex Desire in Film and Television*. New York: Harrington Park Press, 2006.

Dogme 95. "Manifesto"; "Vow of Chastity." Reprinted in *Purity and Provocation: Dogme 95*, edited by Mette Hjort and Scott MacKenzie, 199–200. London: British Film Institute, 2003.

Donner, Jörn. *The Films of Ingmar Bergman: From Torment to All These Women*. Translated by Holger Lundbergh. New York: Dover, 1972.

Doxtater, Amanda. "Bodies in Elevators: The Conveyance of Ethnicity in Recent Swedish Films." In *Northern Constellations: New Readings in Nordic Cinema*, edited by C. Claire Thomas, 59–77. Norwich, UK: Norvik Press, 2006.

Driesel, Birgitta Tollan. "Tystnadens historia." *Bang: Feministisk kulturtidskrift* 1 (1991): 30–33.

Durbin, Karen. "When Love Thought It Could Defeat War." *The New York Times*, August 19, 2001.

Dyer, Richard. *Now You See It: Studies in Lesbian and Gay Film.* 2nd ed. London: Routledge, 2003 [1990].

Elkington, Trevor. "Costumes, Adolescence, and Dogma: Nordic Film and American Distribution." In *Transnational Cinema in a Global North: Nordic Cinema in Transition*, edited by Andrew Nestingen and Trevor Elkington, 31–54. Detroit, MI: Wayne State University Press, 2002.

Elkington, Trevor, and Andrew Nestingen. "Introduction. Transnational Nordic Cinema." In *Transnational Cinema in a Global North: Nordic Cinema in Transition*, edited by Andrew Nestingen and Trevor Elkington, 1–28. Detroit, MI: Wayne State University Press, 2002.

Elsaesser, Thomas. *European Cinema: Face to Face with Hollywood.* Amsterdam: Amsterdam University Press, 2005.

Eskilsson, Tomas. "Att leda regionala utvecklingsprocesser." In *Att Mobilisera för regional tillväxt. Regionala utvecklingsprocesser, kluster och innovationssystem*, edited by Lars Christensen and Peter Kempinsky, 89–106. Lund: Studentlitteratur, 2004.

Esping, Ingrid. "Terrorister—en film om dom dömda: Subjektiva upplevelser av våld och orätt efter Göteborgskravallerna." In *Solskenslandet: Svensk film på 2000-talet*, 221–44. Malmö: Atlantis, 2006.

European Commission. *The European Agenda for Culture.* 2007. http://ec.europa.eu/culture/our-policy-development/doc399_en.htm (accessed April 12, 2010).

Feinberg, Leslie. *Stone Butch Blues: A Novel.* Ann Arbor, MI: Firebrand Books, 1993.

Film i Väst. *Film Factory: Film i Väst 1992–2002.* Edited and text by Marit Kapla. Trollhättan: Film i Väst, 2002.

———. *Filmfabriken: Film i Väst 1992–2002.* Edited and text by Marit Kapla. Trollhättan: Film i Väst, 2002.

Florin, Bo. "Den nationella stilen. Studier i den svenska filmens guldålder." PhD diss., Stockholm University, 1997.

Florin, Ola, Daniel Lundquist, Eva Stenstam, and Klas Viklund, eds. *Vad har mitt liv med Lilja att göra?* Stockholm: Svenska Filminstitutet, 2004.

Forbes, Jill, and Sarah Street. *European Cinema: An Introduction*. London: Palgrave, 2001.

Foster, Gwendolyn Audrey. "Feminist Theory and the Performance of Lesbian Desire in *Persona*." In *Ingmar Bergman's "Persona"*, edited by Lloyd Michaels, 130–45. Cambridge: Cambridge University Press, 1999.

French, Philip. "Swedish teenagers fall in love in the most surprising places..." *The Observer* (London), March 5, 2000.

Fuchs, Oliver. "Das Lange Warten auf die grosse Flatter." *Die Welt*, December 2, 1999.

"Fucking Amal." *Le Point* (Paris), June 2, 2000.

Furhammar, Leif. *Filmen i Sverige: En Historia i Tio Kapitel och en fortsättning*. 3rd ed. Stockholm: Dialogos, 2003.

Galt, Rosalind. *The New European Cinema: Redrawing the Map*. New York: Columbia University Press, 2006.

Gates, Anita. "In a Swedish Town, Girls Will Be Girls." *The New York Times*, October 15, 1999.

Geijerstam, Eva. "After Bergman: New Directions in Swedish Film." In *Film in Sweden*, edited by Francesco Bono and Maaret Koskinen, 43–68. Stockholm: The Swedish Institute, 1996.

Gilbey, Ryan. "A Hole in My Heart." *Sight and Sound*, February 2005. http://www.bfi.org.uk/sightandsound/review/589/ (accessed April 12, 2010).

Göransson, Mattias. "Efter Fucking Åmål." *Dagens Nyheter Lördag Söndag*, August 19, 2000.

Groen, Rick. "Girl Meets Girl Story's Pitch-Perfect Hormone Hell." *The Globe and Mail*, October 29, 1999.

Gustafsson, Annika. "Hem till byn." *Sydsvenska dagbladet*, October 23, 1998.

Halberstam, Judith. *In a Queer Time and Place: Transgender Bodies, Subcultural Lives*. New York: New York University Press, 2005.

Hammar, Thomas. "Closing the Door to the Swedish Welfare State." In

Mechanisms of Immigration Control: A Comparative Analysis of European Regulation Policies, edited by Grete Brochmann and Thomas Hammar, 169–201. Oxford, UK: Berg, 1999.

Hansell, Sven. "Du Är Inte Normal! Kön, Norm Och Frihet i Lukas Moodyssons Filmer." *Kvinnovetenskaplig tidskrift* 25, no. 1/2 (2004): 99–112.

———. "Genusordningar i Lukas Moodyssons Filmer." *Nationellt Seminarium Om Mansforskning*: Report from a symposium 11–12 March 2003. N.p.: Nationellt Seminarium om Mansforskning, 2004. 111–23.

Hedling, Erik. "Breaking the Swedish Sex Barrier: Painful Lustfulness in Ingmar Bergman's *The Silence*." *Film International* 36, no. 6 (2008): 17–27.

———. "The Welfare State Depicted: Post-Utopian Landscapes in Ingmar Bergman's Films." In *Ingmar Bergman Revisited: Performance, Cinema, and the Arts*, edited by Maaret Koskinen, 180–90. London: Wallflower, 2008.

Hedling, Olof. "A New Deal in European Film? Notes on the Swedish Regional Production Turn." *Film International* 35 (2007): 8–17.

———. "Om *"Lilja 4-Ever"*—En Svensk Film." In *Från Eden Till Damavdelningen: Studier Om Kvinnan i Litteraturen: En Vänbok Till Christina Sjöblad*, edited by Bibi Jonsson, Karin Nykvist, and Birthe Sjöberg, 323–34. Absalon: Skrifter utgivna vid Litteraturvetenskapliga institutionen i Lund, 2004.

———. "'Sveriges Mest Kända Korvkiosk': Om regionaliseringen av svensk film." In *Solskenslandet: Svensk Film på 2000-Talet*, edited by Erik Hedling and Ann-Kristin Wallengren, 19–50. Malmö: Atlantis, 2006.

Helgesson, Paulina. "Heteronormativiteten i Receptionshistorien / Paulina Helgesson, Tiina Rosenberg, Raimund Wolfert." *Lambda nordica* 6, no. 4 (2000): 6–53.

Hellman, Cyrill. *Stefan Jarl: En intervjubok*. Stockholm: Kartago, 2008.

Higson, Andrew. "Re-presenting the National Past: Nostalgia and Pastiche in the Heritage Film." In *Fires Were Started: British Cinema and*

Thatcherism, edited by Lester Friedman, 109–29. Minneapolis: Minnesota University Press, 1993.

Hirdman, Yvonne. "Social Engineering and the Woman Question: Sweden in the 1930s." In *Swedish Social Democracy: A Model in Transition*, edited by Wallace Clement and Rianne Mahon, 65–79. Toronto: Canadian Scholars' Press, 1994.

———. "The Social Engineers, the Rationalist Utopia, and the New Home of the 1930s." *International Journal of Political Economy* 22, no. 2 (1992): 27–49.

Hjort, Mette. "From Epiphanic Culture to Circulation: The Dynamics of Globalization in Nordic Cinema." In *Transnational Cinema in a Global North: Nordic Cinema in Transition*, edited by Trevor Elkington and Andrew Nestingen, 191–218. Detroit, MI: Wayne State University Press, 2005.

———. *Lone Scherfig's* Italian for Beginners. Seattle: University of Washington Press, 2010.

———. *Small Nation, Global Cinema: The New Danish Cinema*. Minneapolis: University of Minnesota Press, 2005.

Hoberman, J. "A Squalid Swedish Porno Drama Punishes Its Audience." *The Village Voice*, March 29, 2005.

Howell, Peter. "Girl Meets Girl in Coming-of-Age Tale." *The Toronto Star*, October 29, 1999.

Hynes, Eric. "Review: Distant Voices, Shrill Lives: Lukas Moodysson's *Mammoth*." *Indiewire*, November 16, 2009. http://www.indiewire.com/article/review_distant_voices_shrill_lives_lukas_Moodyssons_mammoth/ (accessed April 12, 2010).

Inside the Head of Lukas Moodysson: The Container Crypt. Art Exhibit. Institute of Contemporary Art. London. http://www.ica.org.uk/Inside%20the%20Head%20of%20Lukas%20Moodysson%3A%20The%20Container%20Crypt+12073.twl (accessed April 12, 2010).

Internet Movie Database. http://www.imdb.com/ (accessed April 12, 2010).

Jacob, Antoine. "Lukas Moodysson, cinéaste citoyen." *Le Monde* (Paris), April 21, 2003.
Jäckel, Anne. *European Film Industries*. London: British Film Institute, 2003.
James, Nick. "Berlin Film Festival." *The Observer* (London), February 15, 2009.
Janson, Malena. "Elvis! Elvis!" In *The Cinema of Scandinavia*, edited by Tytti Soila, 171–79. London: Wallflower, 2005.
———. "Moodysson kan bättre." *Svenska Dagbladet*, January 22, 2009.
———. "Sjuttiotalet är en rolig värld att dyka ner i." *Svenska Dagbladet*, August 16, 2000.
Jensen, Erik. "Moralen helt i halsen." *Politiken* (Copenhagen), February 10, 2009.
Keating, Michael. "Europeanism and Regionalism." In *The European Union and the Regions*, edited by Barry J. Jones and Michael Keating, 1–22. New York: Clarendon Press, 1995.
Kirkland, Bruce. "Swedish Film Shows Us Love." *Toronto Sun*, October 1999.
Koskinen, Maaret. *Ingmar Bergman's "The Silence": Pictures in the Typewriter, Writings on the Screen*. Seattle: University of Washington Press, 2009.
———. "The Swedish Film of the Eighties and Nineties: A Critical Survey." In *Film in Sweden*, edited by Francesco Bono and Maaret Koskinen, 9–42. Stockholm: The Swedish Institute, 1996.
Kristensen, Lars. "Divergent Accounts of Equivalent Narratives: Russian-Swedish *Interdevochka* Meets Swedish-Russian *Lilya 4-ever*." *Portal: Journal of Multidisciplinary International Studies* 4, no. 2 (2007): 1–22.
Kulick, Don, ed. *Queersverige*. Stockholm: Natur och Kultur, 2005.
Lane, Anthony. "Feelings." *New Yorker*, April 11, 2005.
Larsson, Mariah. "Om Kön, Sexualitet Och Moral i *Ett Hål i Mitt Hjärta*." In *Solskenslandet: Svensk Film på 2000-Talet*, 245–67. Malmö: Atlantis, 2006.

Lauer, Andy. "Cinemadaily: '*Mammoth*' Letdown." *Indiewire*, November 20, 2009. http://www.indiewire.com/article/cinemadaily_mammoth_letdown/ (accessed April 12, 2010).

Leigh, Danny. "Lukas Moodysson at the NFT." *The Guardian* (London), November 20, 2002. (This interview is also available as an extra on the UK-released DVD of *Lilya 4-ever*.)

Lindqvist, Ursula. "The Cultural Archive of the IKEA Store." *Space and Culture* 12, no. 1 (2009): 43–62.

Lindskog, Annika. "Sweden in the Eye of the Beholder: Colin Nutley's House of Angels and Swedish Identity." *Scandinavica: An International Journal of Scandinavian Studies* 44, no. 2 (2005): 162–82.

Löfgren, Mikael, and Masoud Vatankhah, eds. *Vad hände med Sverige i Göteborg?* Stockholm: Ordfront, 2002.

Lövin, Isabella. "Drömfabriken c/o Trollhättan." *Månadsjournalen*, February 2001, 36–43.

Lowenstein, Stephen. "Lukas Moodysson: *Show Me Love*." In *My First Move Take Two: Ten Celebrated Directors Talk About Their First Film*, edited by Stephen Lowenstein, 202–21. New York: Pantheon, 2008.

Ludvigsson, Bo. "Starkt och modigt om att finna sitt liv." *Svenska Dagbladet*, October 23, 1998.

Lundquist, Daniel, and Klas Viklund. *"Lilja 4-Ever" på Skolbio: Dokumentation av Svenska Filminstitutets Insatser Kring "Lilja 4-Ever" på Skolbio i Sverige 2003–2004*. Stockholm: Svenska Filminstitutet, 2005.

Mallan, Kerry. "Feeling a Little Queer? Performing Lesbian Desire and Identity in Youth Texts." In *Seriously Playful: Genre, Performance and Text*, edited by Kerry Mallan and Sharyn Pearce, 113–21. Flaxton, Queensland: Post Pressed, 2004.

Mandelbaum, Jacques. "Fucking Åmål: Film Suédois de Lukas Moodysson." *Le Monde* (Paris), June 7, 2000.

Markowitz, Fran. *Coming of Age in Post-Soviet Russia*. Urbana: University of Illinois Press, 2000.

Michelsen, Liselotte. "Teenage-land Retur." *Politiken* (Copenhagen), March 19, 1999.
Miller, Toby. *Global Hollywood*. London: British Film Institute, 2001.
———. *Global Hollywood 2*. London: British Film Institute, 2005.
Moeller, Hans Joergen. "Hjertekvaler i Sovebyen." *Politiken* (Copenhagen), March 12, 1999.
Moodysson, Lukas. *Apo Kryp Hos*. Stockholm: Wahlström och Widstrand, 2006.
———. *Container*. Umeå: Atrium, 2009.
———. *Containermuseum*. Art Installation. Stockholm: Färgfabriken, March, 2006. http://www.fargfabriken.se/index.php?tabell=content&id=78&imgnr=3 (accessed April 12, 2010).
———. *Döden & jag*. Stockholm: Wahlström och Widstrand, 2011.
———. *Det spelar ingen roll var blixtarna slår ner*. Stockholm: Wahlström och Widstrand, 1987.
———. "Detta är den värld vi lever i." In *Vad har mitt liv med Lilja att göra?*, edited by Ola Florin, Daniel Lundquist, Eva Stenstam, and Klas Viklund, 91. Stockholm: Svenska Filminstitutet, 2004.
———. *En vacker sjuk plats*. Stockholm: Wahlström och Widstrand, 2012.
———. "Ett pressmeddelande." Trollhättan: October 18, 1999.
———. *Evangelium enligt Lukas Moodysson*. Stockholm: Wahlström och Widstrand, 1989.
———. *Fucking Åmål*. Stockholm: Bokförlaget DN/Memfis, 1998.
———. "Jag gör filmer för att väcka människor som sover." In *Vad har mitt liv med Lilja att göra?*, edited by Ola Florin, Daniel Lundquist, Eva Stenstam, and Klas Viklund, 13–14. Stockholm: Svenska Filminstitutet, 2004.
———. *Kött*. Stockholm: Wahlström och Widstrand, 1991.
———. *Och andra dikter*. Stockholm: Wahlström och Widstrand, 1988.
———. *Mellan sexton och tjugosex*. Stockholm: Wahlström och Widstrand, 2001.

———. "My desperate teenagers." Interview with Lukas Moodysson. August 30, 2002. www.cineurope.org.

———. *Vad gör jag här: En dikt*. Stockholm: Wahlström och Widstrand, 2002.

———. *Vitt blod*. Stockholm: Wahlström och Widstrand, 1990.

Morrow, Fiona. "Cool Hand Lukas." *The Independent* (London), July 6, 2001.

Mottram, James. "A Hole in My Heart." *Film Review* 653 (2005): 104.

Mulvey, Laura. "Visual Pleasure and Narrative Cinema." In *The Feminism and Visual Culture Reader*, edited by Amelia Jones, 44–53. London: Routledge, 2003.

Nestingen, Andrew K. *Crime and Fantasy in Scandinavia: Fiction, Film, and Social Change*. Seattle: University of Washington Press, 2008.

Neumann, Per, and Charlotte Appelgren. *The Fine Art of Co-Producing*, 2nd ed. Copenhagen: Neumann Publishing, 2007.

"The New Country." http://en.wikipedia.org/wiki/The_New_Country (accessed April 12, 2010).

Nikolajevna, Karin. "Fucking Åmål—Varför En Succé? : En Litteraturvetares Syn på Saken." In *Talandets Lust Och Vånda*, edited by Britt Backlund, 89–101. Lund: Studentlitteratur, 2000.

Noh, David. "Hardcore Spiritualism: Sweden's Lukas Moodysson Explores Personal Vision in *Lilya 4-Ever*." *Film Journal International* 106, no. 5 (2003): 18–20.

Norberg, Martin, and Klas Ekman. *Broder Daniel: When We Were Winning*. Stockholm: Telegram Förlag, 2009.

Ohlson, Elisabeth. Ecce Homo. Photography exhibit. 1998. http://www.ohlson.se/utstallningar_ecce.htm.

Oskarson, Mikael. "Lag eller ordning? Polisens hantering av EU-toppmötet i Göteborg 2001." PhD diss., Stockholm Universitet, 2005.

Pidduck, Julianne. "After 1980: Margins and Mainstreams." In *Now You See It: Studies in Lesbian and Gay Film*, edited by Richard Dyer with Julianne Pidduck, 265–94. 2nd ed. London: Routledge, 2003.

Pred, Allan. *Even in Sweden: Racisms, Racialized Spaces, and the Popular Geographical Imagination.* Berkeley: University of California Press, 2000.

Quinn, Anthony. "The Arts." *The Independent* (London), March 3, 2000.

Qvist, Per Olov. *Folkhemmets Bilder: Modernisering, Motstånd och Mentalitet i Den Svenska 30-Talsfilmen.* Lund: Arkiv, 1995.

———. "Jorden är vår arvedel. Landsbygden i svensk spelfilm 1940–1959." PhD diss., Stockholm University, 1986.

Qvist, Per Olov, and Tytti Soila. "Eva den ustötta/Swedish and underage." In *The Cinema of Scandinavia*, edited by Tytti Soila, 151–58. London: Wallflower, 2005.

"Raus aus Åmål." *Der Spiegel*, November 29, 1999.

Rayns, Tony. "*Lilya 4-ever.*" Film review. *Sight and Sound* 13, no. 5 (2003): 56–58.

Regionerna i centrum. Stockholm: Svenska Filminstitutet, 2001.

Reynolds, Stephanie. "Lesbian Love Story a High School Classic." *The Daily Yomiuri* (Tokyo), May 18, 2000.

Rich, Ruby. "New Queer Cinema." In *New Queer Cinema: A Critical Reader*, edited by Michele Aaron, 15–22. Edinburgh: Edinburgh University Press, 2004.

Rivi, Luisa. *European Cinema After 1989,* New York: Palgrave Macmillan, 2007.

Rosenberg, Tiina. "Det Nya Lukas-Evangeliet: Om Det Heteronormativa Mottagandet Av Fucking Åmål." *Lambda nordica* 6, no. 4 (2000): 23–36.

Rugg, Linda Haverty. "Gender and Sex in Scandinavian Cinema as Screened in the American Mind." In *Bent: Gender and Sexuality in Contemporary Scandinavian Art*, edited by Whitney Chadwick, 34–39. San Francisco: International Center for the Arts at San Francisco State University, 2006.

Sarikakis, Katharine. *Media and Cultural Policy in the European Union.* Amsterdam: Rodopi, 2007.

Schembi, Jim. "Fragile Teens handled without mockery." *The Age* (Melbourne), December 22, 2000.

Scott, Kevin Conroy. "Lukas Moodysson: *Together.*" In *Screenwriters' Masterclass: Screenwriters Talk About Their Greatest Movies*, edited by Kevin Conroy Scott, 244–65. London: Faber and Faber, 2005.

Sedgwick, Eve Kosofsky. *Epistemology of the Closet*. 2nd ed. Berkeley: University of California Press, 2008 [1990].

Seidel, Hans-Dieter. "Raus aus Åmål." *Frankfurter Allgemeine Zeitung*, December 4, 1999.

Shary, Timothy. *Teen Movies: American Youth on Screen*. London: Wallflower Press, 2005.

"Skål för Åmål." *Expressen* (Stockholm), October 28, 1993.

Skugge, Linda Norrman. "Varför tiger recensenterna om lesbisk kärlek." *Expressen* (Stockholm), December 12, 1998.

Soila, Tytti, Astrid Söderbergh Widding, and Gunnar Iversen. "Introduction: Film Production as a National Project." In *Nordic National Cinemas*, edited by Tytti Soila, Astrid Söderbergh Widding, and Gunnar Iversen, 1–6. London: Routledge, 1998.

Sparrmann, Anna. "Film as a Political and Educational Device: Talk about Men, Male Sexuality and Gender among Swedish Youth." *Visual Studies* 21, no. 2 (2006): 167–82.

Steene, Birgitta, with Eva Norin. *Måndagar med Bergman: En svensk publik möter Ingmar Bergmans filmer*. Stockholm/Stehag: Brutus Östlings Bokförlag Symposion, 1996.

Stenport, Anna Westerståhl, and Cecilia Alm. "Corporations, Crime, and Gender Construction in Stieg Larsson's *The Girl with the Dragon Tattoo*: Exploring Twenty-First Century Neoliberalism in Swedish Culture." *Scandinavian Studies* 81, no. 2 (2009): 157–78.

Stone, Jay. "Familiar Story Beautifully Told." *The Ottawa Citizen*, November 26, 1999.

Stuart, Jamie. *Performing Queer Female Identity on Screen: A Critical Analysis of Five Recent Films*. N.p.: McFarland & Company, 2008.

Sundholm, Magnus. "*Tillsammans* tredje bästa film i USA." *Arbetet*, December 15, 2001.

Svanström, Yvonne. "En självklar efterfrågan." In *Vad har mitt liv med Lilja att göra?*, edited by Ola Florin, Daniel Lundquist, Eva Stenstam, and Klas Viklund, 45–57. Stockholm: Svenska Filminstitutet, 2004.

Svenberg, Jenny. "Tack Gud att jag är lesbisk: Om homosexualitet." In *Fittstim*, edited by Linda Norrman Skugge, Belinda Olsson, and Brita Zilg, 102–11. Stockholm: Bokförlaget DN, 1999.

Svensk filmdatabas. Svenska Filminstitutet. http://www.sfi.se/en-gb/Swedish-film-database/ (accessed April 12, 2010).

Sweet, Matthew. "Bought and Sold? Lukas Moodysson's Acclaimed New Film *Lilya 4-ever*." *The Independent* (London), March 28, 2003.

Thunberg, Karin. "Vart tog deras lesbiska kärlek vägen?" *Svenska Dagbladet*, December 12, 1998.

Tigervall, Cecilia. "Folkhemsk film med 'invandraren' i rollen som den sympatiske Andre." PhD diss., Umeå University, 2005.

Timm, Mikael. *Dröm och förbannad verklighet: Spelet om svensk film under 40 år*. Stockholm: Svenska Filminstitutet, 2003.

United Nations. Committee on the Elimination of Racial Discrimination. *Twelfth periodic reports of States parties due in 1995. Addendum. Sweden*. October 25, 1996.

Wallengren, Ann-Kristin. "Kultur och Okultur—Bilden Av Landsbygdens Folk." In *Solskenslandet: Svensk Film på 2000-Talet*, edited by Erik Hedling and Ann-Kristin Wallengren, 51–80. Malmö: Atlantis, 2006.

Walling, James. "The Poetry of Pain." *The Prague Post*, March 17, 2010.

Wanner, Catherine, and Mark Steinberg. "Introduction: Reclaiming the Sacred After Communism." In *Religion, Morality, and Community in Post-Soviet Aesthetics*, edited by Mark D. Steinberg and Catherine Wanner, 1–20. Washington, DC: Woodrow Wilson Center Press; Bloomington: Indiana University Press, 2008.

Weman, Mats. "Lukas Moodysson." Interview. In *Regionerna i centrum*, 26–27. Stockholm: Svenska Filminstitutet, 2001.

———. "Pastor Moodyssons Bekännelser." *Nöjesguiden*, September 9, 2000.
Wennerholm, Carolina Johansson. "Crossing Borders and Bridges: The Baltic Region Networking Project." *Gender and Development* 10, no. 1 (2002): 10–19.
Wennö, Nicholas. "Radikal filmarduo låter aktivisterna tala ut." *Dagens Nyheter*, June 18, 2003.
Werner, Jeff. *Medelvägens estetik. Sverigebilder i USA*. Vol. 2. Hedemora: Gidlunds, 2008.
Whatling, Clare. *Screen Dream: Fantasising Lesbians in Film*. Manchester: Manchester University Press, 1997.
Widerberg, Bo. *Visionen i svensk film*. Stockholm: Bonnier, 1962.
Wilson, Roger. "Sista Föreställningen." *Fokus* 35 (2006): 24–33.
Wood, Mary P. *Contemporary European Cinema*. London: Hodder Arnold, 2007.
Wright, Rochelle. "'Immigrant Film' in Sweden at the Millenium." In *Transnational Cinema in a Global North: Nordic Cinema in Transition*, edited by Trevor Elkington and Andrew Nestingen, 55–72. Detroit, MI: Wayne State University Press, 2005.
Yellowbird Productions. http://www.yellowbird.se (accessed November 13, 2009).
Zern, Leif. *Se Bergman*. Stockholm: Norstedts, 1993.

Filmography

Akerman, Chantal. *Je, tu, il, elle*. World Artists, 1977.
Almodóvar, Pedro. *All About My Mother (Todo sobre mi madre)*. Sony Pictures Classics, 1999.
Andersson, Roy. *A Love Story (En Kärlekshistoria)*. Europa Film, 1970.
Apelgren, Stephan. *Sune's Christmas (Sunes Jul)*. Svensk Television, 1991.
Axel, Gabriel. *Babette's Feast (Babettes gæstebud)*. Orion Classics, 1988.
Bagher, Reza. *Popular Music from Vittula (Populärmusic från Vittula)*. Svensk filmindustri, 2004.
———. *Wings of Glass (Vingar av glas)*. Chimney Pot, 2000.
Baker, Roy Ward. *The Vampire Lovers*. American International Pictures, 1970.
Bergman, Ingmar. *Cries and Whispers (Viskningar och rop)*. Svensk filmindustri, 1973.
———. *Fanny and Alexander (Fanny och Alexander)*. Svensk filmindustri, 1982.
———. *Persona*. Svensk filmindustri, 1966.
———. *Scenes From a Marriage. (Scener ur ett äktenskap)*. Svensk filmindustri, 1973.
———. *Serpent's Egg (Ormens ägg)*. Paramount, 1977.

———. *The Silence* (*Tystnaden*). Svensk filmindustri, 1963.
———. *Summer With Monika* (*Sommaren med Monika*). Svensk filmindustri, 1953.
———. *Three Strange Loves* (*Törst*). Svensk filmindustri, 1949.
———. *Through a Glass Darkly* (*Såsom i en spegel*). Svensk filmindustri, 1961.
———. *Winter Light* (*Nattvardsgästerna*). Svensk filmindustri, 1963.
Blom, Maria. *Dalecarlians* (*Masdjävlar*). Memfis, 2004.
———. *Fishy*. Memfis, 2008.
Brickman, Paul. *Risky Business*. Warner Brothers, 1983.
Cameron, James. *Titanic*. Paramount Pictures, 1997.
Carpenter, John. *Halloween*. Compass International Pictures, 1978.
Cassavetes, John. *The Killing of a Chinese Bookie*. Faces Distribution, 1976.
Clark, Larry. *Kids*. Shining Excalibur Films, 1995.
Craven, Wes. *A Nightmare on Elm Street*. New Line Cinema, 1984.
Cunningham, Sean. *Friday the 13th*. Paramount Pictures, 1980.
Dahlström, Alexandra. *Because the Night*. Bob Film, 2009.
Dmytryk, Edward. *A Walk on the Wild Side*. Columbia Pictures, 1962.
Dreyer, Carl Theodor. *Mikael*. Universum Film, 1924.
———. *Master of the House* (*Du skal ære din hustru*). Palladium Film, 1925.
Eastwood, Clint. *Midnight in the Garden of Good and Evil*. Warner Brothers, 1997.
Fares, Josef. *Jalla! Jalla!* Memfis, 2000.
———. *Kopps!* Memfis, 2003.
———. *Zozo*. Memfis, 2005.
Ganslandt, Jesper. *The Ape*. Fasad, 2009.
Gilbert, Brian. *Wilde*. Sony Pictures Classics, 1997.
Gorris, Marleen. *Antonia*. First Look International, 1995.
Hallström, Lasse. *My Life as a Dog*. (*Mitt liv som hund*). Svensk filmindustri, 1987.

Haynes, Todd. *Poison*. Zeitgeist, 1991.
——. *Velvet Goldmine*. Miramax, 1998.
Heckerling, Amy. *Fast Times at Ridgemont High*. Universal Pictures, 1982.
Hughes, John. *The Breakfast Club*. Universal Pictures, 1985.
——. *Pretty in Pink*. Paramount, 1986.
——. *Sixteen Candles*. Universal Pictures, 1984.
——. *Some Kind of Wonderful*. Paramount, 1987.
Kalin, Tom. *Swoon*. Fine Line, 1992.
Keining, Alexandra. *With Every Heartbeat (Kyss mig)*. Lebox Produktion, 2011.
Kurys, Diane. *Coup de Foudre (Entre Nous)*. Gaumont, 1983.
——. *Peppermint Soda (Diabolo Menthe)*. Gaumont, 1977.
Lagerlöf, Daniel Lind. *His and Hers (Hans och Hennes)*. Hägring, 2001.
Livingstone, Jennie. *Paris Is Burning*. Miramax, 1990.
Macdonald, Hettie. *Beautiful Thing*. Sony Pictures Classics, 1996.
Maggenti, Maria. *The Incredibly True Adventure of Two Girls in Love*. Fine Line Features, 1995.
Malmros, Ulf. *Slim Susie (Smala Sussie)*. Götafilm, 2003.
Martin, Philip. *Sidetracked*; *Firewall*; *One Step Behind*. BBC. PBS. 2008. Television series.
Mattson, Arne. *One Summer of Happiness (Hon dansade en sommar)*. Svensk filmindustri, 1951.
Memfis. Box-set of DVDs. Stockholm, 2009.
Memfis. *Memfis Shorts*. DVD. Stockholm, 2009.
Moodysson, Lukas. *Container*. Memfis DVD, 2006.
——. *En uppgörelse i den undre världen (Settlement in the Underworld)*. Stockholm: Dramatiska institutet, 1996.
——. *A Hole in My Heart (Ett Hål i Mitt Hjärta)*. Memfis DVD, 2005. Distributor in Sweden: Sonet; in the US: Newmarket Films, 2009.
——. *Lilya 4-ever (Lilja 4-ever)*. Memfis DVD, 2002. Distributor in Sweden: Sonet; in the US: Newmarket Films, 2009.

———. *Mammoth* (*Mammut*). Memfis DVD, 2009. Distributor in Sweden: Svensk filmindustri; in the US: IFC Films, 2009.

———. *Show Me Love* (*Fucking Åmål*). Memfis DVD, 1998. Distributor in Sweden: Sonet; in the US: Strand Releasing. Film, 2009 (DVD includes a track with director's comments in Swedish).

———. *Talk* (*Bara prata lite*). Memfis, 1997 (reissued in the DVD *Memfis Shorts*, 2009).

———. *Together* (*Tillsammans*). Memfis DVD, 2000. Distributor in Sweden: Sonet Film; in the US: IFC Films, 2009.

Moodysson, Lukas, and Peter Birro. Screenplay. *The New Country* (*Det nya landet*). Swedish Television, 2000. Four-part television series.

———. Screenplay. *The New Country* (*Det nya landet*). Göta Film, 2000. Feature film.

Moodysson, Lukas, and Stefan Jarl. *The Kids They Sentenced* (*Terrorister: En film om dom dömda*). Folkets Bio, 2003.

Moreton, David. *Edge of Seventeen*. Strand Releasing, 1998.

Nutley, Colin. *House of Angels* (*Änglagård*). Sony Pictures Classics, 1992.

O'Haver, Tommy. *Billy's Hollywood Screen Kiss*. Trimark Pictures, 1998.

Pollack, Kay. *As It Is in Heaven* (*Så som i himmelen*). Sonet Film, 2004.

Scott, Tony. *The Hunger*. MGM/UA, 1983.

Sjöman, Vilgot. *I am Curious Yellow* (*Jag är nyfiken gul*). Svensk filmindustri, 1967.

Sjöström, Victor. *The Outlaw and His Wife* (*Berg-Ejvind och hans hustru*). Svenska biografteatern, 1918.

Stiller, Mauritz. *Sir Arne's Treasure* (*Herr Arnes pengar*). Svenska bios Filmbyrå, 1919.

Sundvall, Kjell. *The Guy in the Grave Next Door* (*Grabben i graven brevid*). Filmlance International, 2002.

Taslimi, Susan. *All Hell Let Loose* (*Hus i helvete*). Film i Väst, 2002.

Troell, Jan. *Hamsun*. Svensk filmindustri, 1996.

Truffaut, François. *The 400 Blows* (*Les quatre cents coups*). Les Films du Carrosse, 1959.

Van Sant, Gus. *My Own Private Idaho*. Fine Line Cinemas, 1991.
Verhoeven, Paul. *Basic Instinct*. TriStar Pictures, 1992.
Vinterberg, Thomas. *The Celebration (Festen)*. Unattributed director Thomas Vinterberg. October Films, 1998.
Von Trier, Lars. *Breaking the Waves*. October Films, 1996.
———. *Dancer in the Dark*. Fine Line Features, 2000.
———. *Dogville*. Lions Gate Films, 2003.
———. *The Idiots*. *(Idioterne)*. Unattributed director Lars von Trier. Zentropa, 1998.
———. *Manderlay*. IFC Films, 2005.

Index

Page numbers in italics refer to illustrations.

Aaron, Michele, 75
ABBA, 37
Ace of Base, 37
adolescence/childhood (as film theme): adolescent sexual ambivalence theme, 9, 44; children as social critics, 4–5, 124; coming-of-age/coming-out theme, 3, 31, 74, 90–91; high school films, 31–32, 76–77, 81, 89–90; independent children as Swedish theme, 53; small town life and, 100–101; in Swedish film, 53, 89–90; teen movie genre, 76–77, 90–91
Ahlberg, Anna Malini, 17, 104
Åhlund, Jannike, 4
Akerman, Chantal, 74
Akinshina, Oksana, 21

All About My Mother (Pedro Almodóvar, 1999), 74
Almodóvar, Pedro, 74
Åmål, Sweden (*Show Me Love* setting), 34, 83–84, 91, 99–103
ambivalence (as Moodysson theme): overview, 6–8; authenticity and, 13; heteronormative practices in *Show Me Love*, 152n49; political vs. aesthetic voicing in *Kids They Sentenced*, 128; sexual ambivalence in *Show Me Love*, 44, 46, 55, 56; spatiality as device for, 9
Andersson, Bibi, 55
Andersson, Roy, 6, 78
Antonia (Marlene Gorris, 1995), 74
Åsberg, Josefin, 17
Assmo, Per, 110

auteur filmmaking paradigm,
  15–16, 19, 26, 53–54, 151n42
authenticity: adolescents as vehicle for, 21; ambivalence and, 13; dialogue as role in, 19; Dogme 95 cinematic style, 50; everyday situations as Moodysson theme, 5–6; lesbian theme as spectacle vs. reality, 74–75; Moodysson rejection of commercialism, 11; place/locality as source of, 22–23, 99–103; in Swedish and European film, 8–9; Swedish cultural stereotypes and, 90; Trollhättan production environment and, 103
awards: *Guldbagge* ceremony of 1999, 11; *Lilya 4-ever* awards, 18, 130, 174n26; *Show Me Love* awards, 3, 11, 32, 36, 141; *Together* awards, 168n2
Axel, Gabriel, 25, 96

Babette's Feast (*Babettes gæstebud*, Gabriel Axel, 1998), 25, 96
Baker, Roy Ward, 75
Basic Instinct (Paul Verhoeven, 1992), 75
Beautiful Thing (Hettie MacDonald, 1996), 76
Benshoff, Harry, 73
Bergman, Ingmar: depiction of landscape in, 94–95; early international distribution, 74; independent children theme in, 53; landscape in, 95; Moodysson comparisons to, 4, 12, 54–55, 89–90; natural light in, 26; *Persona* references in *Show Me Love*, 26, 54–58, 56–57; publication of scripts by, 53; reception in Sweden, 54, 151n40; response to *Show Me Love*, 4; Swedish national cinema and, 112–13
Berlin Film Festival, 32, 88, 108, 132, 134
Billy's Hollywood Screen Kiss (Tommy O'Haver, 1998), 76
Birro, Peter, 4
Björk, 98
Björklund, Jenny, 46, 55, 59, 75, 84
Blom, Maria, 97
Boije af Gennäs, Louise, 63
Bråding, Sanna, 21
Brantås, Ulf, 17–18, 48–52, 57
The Breakfast Club (John Hughes, 1985), 77
Breaking the Waves (Lars von Trier, 1996), 25, 130, 167–68n95
Brickman, Paul, 77
British Film Institute, Sutherland Trophy, 88
Broder Daniel, 63, 68, 72

Bronski, Michael, 76–77
Butler, Judith, 42, 63

Cameron, James, 90
Cannes Film Festival, 108
Carlson, Erica, 66–67
Carlsson, Gunnar, 103
Carpenter, John, 77
Cassavetes, John, 6, 51
casting: amateur/local actors in *Show Me Love*, 65–66; Moodysson avoidance of recasted actors, 20–21; Moodysson production collective, 17–18; Moodysson style of, 6, 20
The Celebration (*Festen*, Thomas Vinterberg, 1998), 46, 47, 94–95
characterization: essentialism in feminine characters, 21–22; ethnic homogeneity in *Show Me Love*, 102; heteronormative characterization in *Show Me Love*, 64; journal writing as device for, 32–33; lesbian characterization in *Show Me Love*, 62–65; use of interior/confinement scenes and, 64–65, 67–68
childhood. *See* adolescence/childhood
Christian tragedy (in *Lilya 4-ever*), 130–31
cinematography: 16-mm format, 47–48; cinemascope aspect ration in *Mammoth*, 136; crash zooms, 18, 51–52; digital video format, 47; documentary techniques, 6, 49–50; Dogme 95 "home movie" production values, 50, 52; establishing shots, 18, 52; gaze as cinematic device, 32, 62; handheld camera aesthetics, 47, 50–51; interior/confinement scenes in *Show Me Love*, 43–44, 47, 48, 50, 64–65, 67–68, 72–73; mirror shots as self-reflexive gaze, 59–62, 61; Moodysson production collective, 17–18; reverse film stock technique, 7, 47, 48–49; widescreen cinemascope aspect ratio, 7. *See also* landscape; lighting
Clark, Larry, 78
class: provincial landscape aesthetic and, 97; *Show Me Love* casting and, 67; *Show Me Love* depiction of, 33, 79–83; Trollhättan as working-class community, 101; working-class lesbian identity, 63–64
collaborative filmmaking, 14–16, 17–19, 104, 133, 176n37
Container (2006): overview, 133–34; childhood as theme of,

5; critical and public reception, 176–77n44; distribution, 17; experimental style in, 4, 12; filming locations, 109, 134; image-soundtrack disconnect in, 7; as low-budget film, 135; transsexualism as theme in, 21–22, 133–34
costume dramas, 25
Coup de foudre (Diane Kurys, 1983), 74
Craven, Wes, 77
Cries and Whispers (*Viskningar och rop*, Ingmar Bergman, 1973), 26–27

Dahlström, Alexandra: acting awards, 3; articulation of desire in *Show Me Love*, 30–31; casting of, 21, 65–67; comparisons to Bibi Andersson, 55, 56–57; as production collective member, 17–19; *Show Me Love* lesbian fans and, 42; as *Show Me Love* script publication feature, 53
Dalecarlians (*Masjävlar*, Maria Blom, 2004), 97
Dancer in the Dark (Lars von Trier, 2000), 25, 97–98
Danish Bodil awards, 88
Danish Film Institute, 16, 117
de Geer, Carl Johan, 125

Dennis, Jeffrey P., 77–78
Denward, Charlotta, 36
dialogue: as basis for Jönsson collaboration, 14–15; foreign language dialogue, 23; as fundamental filmmaking component, 19; improvisation in, 20; Moodysson style of, 6; publication of *Show Me Love* script, 53
documentary film, 6, 49–50. See also *The Kids They Sentenced*
Dogme 95: Moodysson affiliation with, 24–26; production values associated with, 46–47, 50, 52; rejection of aestheticized nature, 94–95; *Show Me Love* association with, 90; storytelling/acting primacy in, 52
Dogville (Lars von Trier, 2003), 25–26, 160n35
Dramatiska Institutet, 11–12, 14, 18, 113–14
Dreyer, Carl Theodor, 26, 169n5
Döden & Co (Death and Company, semi-autobiographical Moodysson narrative, 2011), 5

economy: auteur filmmaking paradigm and, 16; coproduction funding, 161n38; European Union regionalization initiative, 87, 105–11, 121–22; *Mammoth* as big-budget film, 135–36; regional film production centers and, 121; *Show Me Love* financing and box office receipts, 35, 90, 115; transnational film and, 112–17; Trollhättan economic context, 101–2, 120–21

Edge of Seventeen (David Moreton, 1998), 76

Elkington, Trevor, 115–16, 165–66n81

Elsaesser, Thomas, 112–13

Eskilsson, Tomas, 103, 107, 111

Esping, Ingrid, 171n16, 171n18

ethnicity/race, 26, 87, 102, 121, 127

Europa Film, 113–14

European Convention on Cinematographic Coproduction, 116

European film: aestheticized landscape in, 96–98; regional film production centers, 111, 121; same-sex themes in, 74; *Show Me Love* promotion/reception, 43

European Union regionalization initiative, 87, 105–12, 121–22

Fanny and Alexander (*Fanny och Alexander*, Ingmar Bergman, 1982), 27, 53, 146n48

Fares, Josef, 97

Fast Times at Ridgemont High (Amy Heckerling, 1982), 77

Feinberg, Leslie, 63–64

festival screenings: overview, 138–140; Berlin Film Festival, 32, 88, 108, 132, 134; Cannes Film Festival, 108; Karlovy Vary Film Festival, 88; Montreal Film Festival, 88; Toronto Film Festival, 88

Filmhuset, 113–14

filming location. *See* location

Film i Väst: overview, 103–11; founding of, 163n53; Memfis Film collaboration with, 16, 117; *Show Me Love* regionalism theme and, 120–21; *Show Me Love* success and, 86, 147n5; von Trier collaborations with, 97–98, 160n35

Folkets Bio, 128

Forbes, Jill, 112

Fornander, Malin, 17

Forsell, Malte, 17, 69–70

Foster, Gwendolyn Audrey, 58

The 400 Blows (François Truffaut, 1959), 52–53

French, Philip, 92

French New Wave, 52

Friday the 13th (Sean Cunningham, 1980), 77

Furhammar, Leif, 4

Galt, Rosalind, 96, 112
gaze: Bergman references in *Show Me Love*, 58; disruptive cinematic techniques for, 32, 62; mirror shots as self-reflexive gaze, 59–62, 61; queered heteronormative gaze in *Show Me Love*, 28–29, 30–31, 45–46, 58, 71–72
Geijerstam, Eva af, 113
gender: adolescent ambivalence toward gender/sexuality, 9; as Bergman theme, 26–27; critique of Christian tragedy in *Lilya 4-ever*, 130–31; essentialism in feminine characterization, 21–22; female adolescent lives as Moodysson theme, 4–5, 21, 85; feminist reception to *Show Me Love*, 42; heteronormative paradigm in *Show Me Love*, 38, 43, 59, 78–83, 152n49; heteronormativity in high school films, 76–77; Swedish lesbian identity, 63–64; transgender entrapment as *Container* theme, 133–34; women protagonists in Moodysson, 21. *See also* gaze; LGBT film; sexuality
genre, 73–76
Gorris, Marleen, 74
Griffin, Sean, 73

Halberstam, Judith, 46
Halloween (John Carpenter, 1978), 77
Hallström, Lasse, 27, 53, 89
Hamsun (Jan Troell, 1996), 96, 115–16
Hansson, Per Albin, 126
Haynes, Todd, 74
Heckerling, Amy, 77
Hedling, Erik, 93, 95
heritage films, 25, 96
high school films, 31–32, 76–77, 81, 89–90
Hjort, Mette, 112
Hoberman, J., 75
Hole in My Heart, A (*Ett hål i mitt hjärta*, 2005): overview, 132–33; Bergman influence in, 27; casting, 21; chamber play structure in, 27; collaborative production, 133, 176n37; experimental style in, 4, 7, 131–32; filming location, 23, 25–26, 109; pornography as theme in, 21–22, 132; as small-budget film, 132
Hollywood. *See* U.S. film industry
House of Angels (*Änglagård*, Colin Nutley, 1992), 118
Hughes, John, 77
The Hunger (Tony Scott, 1983), 75–76

I Am Curious Yellow (*Jag är nyfiken gul*, Vilgot Sjöman, 1967), 74
Ibsen, Henrik, 148–49n14
The Idiots (*Idioterne*, Lars von Trier, 1998), 25, 46, 94–95
Iversen, Gunnar, 165–66n81

Jarl, Stefan, 4, 6, 27, 54, 127–28, 171n18
Je, tu, il, elle (Chantal Akerman, 1977), 74
Jensen, Peter Aalbaek, 17, 111, 118
Jönsson, Lars: collaborative script revision process, 14–15; on Memfis financing, 117, 167–68n95; Moodysson introduction to, 13–14; *Show Me Love* distribution and, 35–36; Trollhättan production center and, 111
Jörgensen, Geir Hansteen, 127

Kalin, Tom, 74
Karlovy Vary Film Festival, 88
Keating, Michael, 106
Kids (Larry Clark, 1995), 78
The Kids They Sentenced (*Terrorister: En film om dom dömda*, 2003), 4, 54, 127–28, 171n16, 171n18
The Killing of a Chinese Bookie (John Cassavetes, 1976), 51

Kopps! (Josef Fares, 2003), 97
Krusenstjerna, Agnes von, 63
kung fu movies, 51–52
Kurlandsky, Jesper, 17–19
Kurys, Diane, 74

Lagerlöf, Selma, 63
landscape: avoidance in Moodysson and von Trier cinematography, 25–26, 87, 94, 96–98; as component of national identity, 93–96; as feature of Scandinavian cinema, 26, 92–94; provincial landscape aesthetic and, 96–98; in transnational film, 121–22. *See also* cinematography; location
language: language diversity in Moodysson films, 23, 134–35; regional dialect in *Show Me Love*, 35, 66–67; *Show Me Love* title and, 36–38; translations (of films), 20
Larsson, Carl, 93–94
Leigh, Danny, 172–73n20
Leigh, Mike, 6
Leszczylowski, Michal, 17–18, 52, 136, 178n49
LGBT film: "doomed lesbian" formula, 75; heteronormative paradigm in, 38, 41, 59, 61–62, 64–65, 78–83; high school films

and, 31–32, 76–77, 81, 89–90;
lesbian characterization in *Show Me Love*, 62–65; lesbian theme as spectacle vs. reality, 74–75; New Queer Cinema, 3, 74–76; queering strategy in *Show Me Love*, 28–29, 43, 49, 58, 72; reception of *Show Me Love*, 41–42, 89; sisterhood in Moodysson, 58–59. *See also* gender; queering; sexuality

lighting: limited use of filters, 6; natural lighting, 26, 47, 50, 72; in *Show Me Love*, 50, 56–58, 72–73

Liljeberg, Rebecca, 3, 30–31, 30–31, 65–67

Lilya 4-ever (*Lilja 4-ever*, 2002): overview, 128–132; awards, 18, 130, 174n26; casting, 21; children as social critics in, 124; cinematography, 48, 51; distribution, 17; filming location, 109; financing and box office receipts, 4, 174n26; foreign language dialogue in, 20, 23; human trafficking as theme in, 21–22, 127, 172–73n20; place/locality as production design component, 22–23; post-Soviet life as theme, 134; von Trier comparisions and, 25

literary adaptations, 25

Livingstone, Jennie, 74

Loach, Ken, 6

location (setting): Åmål as *Show Me Love* setting, 34, 83–84, 91; delocalization in von Trier, 98, 160n35; Dogme 95 stipulations for, 94–95; European Union regionalization and, 87, 105–11, 121–22; high school setting, 76–77; locality/place and, 22–23, 65–67, 72–73, 99–103; location substitution, 98–103; mundane locations in *Show Me Love*, 34, 94–95; runaway productions, 98; rural/provincial settings, 91–97, 113, 120; small town settings, 84, 86, 92, 96–97, 100–101, 113; spatial ambivalence and, 9, 91–92, 98, 112; Trollhättan as *Show Me Love* filming location, 4, 14, 23, 25–26, 34, 66–67, 72–73, 86. *See also* landscape

Love Story, A (*En kärlekshistoria*, Roy Andersson, 1970), 78

Macdonald, Hettie, 76

Maggenti, Maria, 75–76

Malmöligan (Malmö poetry collective), 10, 14

Mammoth (*Mammut*, 2009):
overview, 134–35; casting, 21;
cinematography, 7, 24; critical
and public reception, 177n46,
178n48; distribution, 17;
editing, 136, 178n49; filming
location, 109; financing and
box office receipts, 4, 135–37,
177n46; foreign language dialogue in, 20, 23; neoliberalism/
transnationalism as theme in,
23–24, 134–35; place/locality
as production design component, 23; script revision process,
14–15; as transnational film,
113

Manderlay (Lars von Trier, 2005),
25, 160n35

Mankell, Henning, 121

Markowitz, Fran, 131

Master of the House (*Du skal
ære din nustru*, Carl Theodor
Dreyer, 1925), 169n5

Mattson, Arne, 74, 94

Memfis Film: collaborative filmmaking and, 15–16, 17–19;
funding resources, 118, 167–
68n95; influence on Moodysson,
116–17; repertory casting and,
14; *Show Me Love* distribution/
marketing, 35–36, 40; transnational productions, 117–18

Miller, Toby, 98, 166n81

mirror shots, 59–62, 61

Montreal Film Festival, 88

Moodysson, Lukas: aesthetic and
affective experimentation, 7,
57–58, 131–32, 133–34; as
auteur-style director, 15–16, 19,
26, 53–54, 151n42; biographical sketch, 10–11; directors who
influenced Moodysson, 6; films
directed by, 4; stature in Swedish culture, 3

Moreton, David, 76

Mulvey, Laura, 29

My Life as a Dog (*Mitt liv som
hund*, Lasse Hallström, 1987),
27, 53, 89

My Own Private Idaho (Gus Van
Sant, 1991), 74

narrative. *See* plot

national identity: European Union
regionalization initiative and,
87, 105–12, 121–22; landscapes and nature imagery
association with, 87, 93–94;
Nordic national cinema, 16, 94,
114–19, 165–66n81; Swedish national cinema, 112–14,
165–66n81

neoliberalism, 23–24, 26–27, 127,
129, 134–35

Nestingen, Andrew, 115–16, 165–66n81
The New Country (Det nya landet, 2000), 4, 127
Newmarket Films, 130
New Queer Cinema, 3, 74–76
Nightmare on Elm Street, A (Wes Craven, 1984), 77
Nordic film, 16, 94, 114–19, 165–66n81
Nordic Film and Television Fund (NFTF), 16, 114–15
Norwegian Amanda Awards, 88
Nutley, Colin, 118
Nykvist, Sven, 26

O'Haver, Tommy, 76
Ohlson, Elizabeth, 41, 149n16
One Summer of Happiness (Hon dansade en sommar, Arne Mattson, 1951), 74, 94
The Outlaw and His Wife (Berg-Ejvind och hans hustru, Victor Sjöstrom, 1918), 93

Paris is Burning (Jennie Livingstone, 1990), 74
Peppermint Soda (Diabolo menthe, Diane Kurys, 1977), 74
Persona (Ingmar Bergman, 1966), 26, 54–58, 56–57, 59–62, 95
plot: establishing shots as technique in, 18; Show Me Love absence of narrative closure, 38; Show Me Love plot synopsis, 34–35; written text and voice-over techniques, 32–33
Poison (Todd Haynes, 1991), 74
political film: ambivalence theme and, 7–8; Kids They Sentenced as political documentary, 127–28, 171n16; Lilya 4-ever as political melodrama, 128–29; post-Soviet life as Moodysson theme, 134; as rejection of aestheticized auteur films, 54; Scandinavia as politically insulated, 26; social realism as Moodysson theme, 27, 84–85; Together as political parody, 124
Possne, Peter, 35–36
Pred, Allan, 101
Pretty in Pink (John Hughes, 1986), 77
production design: documentary techniques, 6, 49–50; Dogme 95 production guideline, 46–47; international filming locations, 22–23; Moodysson attention to detail, 101; Moodysson collaborative production style, 14–16, 17–18, 104, 133, 176n37; place/locality role in, 22–23; produc-

tion-design immersion technique, 7, 73, 169n5; script revision process, 14–15; spatial ambivalence and, 9, 91–92, 98, 112

queering: cinematic techniques and, 49; *Fucking Åmål* as small-town queering, 37–38, 46, 71–72; of the heteronormative gaze in *Show Me Love*, 28–29, 30–31, 45–46, 58, 71–72; queer cultural representation in Sweden, 41–43; *Show Me Love* reception and, 3, 41, 43

reverse film stock technique, 7, 47, 48–49
Rich, Ruby, 74–75
Risky Business (Paul Brickman, 1983), 77
Robyn, 37, 65, 72
Rosenberg, Tiina, 41
runaway productions, 98
Rust, Mathias, 66–67

Sandrew, 113–14, 119
Sauk, Stefan, 14
Scandinavian film, 24–26
Scenes from a Marriage (*Scener ur ett äktenskap*, Ingmar Bergman, 1973), 27
Scherfig, Lone, 24
Scorsese, Martin, 6
Scott, Tony, 75
The Serpent's Egg (*Ormens ägg*, Ingmar Bergman, 1977), 113
set design, 43–44, 47, 48, 50, 64–65, 67–68, 72–73, 153n60
setting. *See* location
sexuality: absence of aestheticized sexuality in *Show Me Love*, 94; adolescent ambivalence as Moodysson theme, 9, 44; as Bergman theme, 26–27; destabilized sexual conventions in *Show Me Love*, 33–34; human trafficking as *Lilya 4-ever* theme, 21–22, 127, 172–73n20; lesbian desire in *Persona*, 58; lesbian desire in *Show Me Love*, 21–22, 28–29, 41–43, 55, 56; masturbation in Bergman and Moodysson, 58–59; pornography as *Hole in My Heart* theme, 21–22, 132; *Show Me Love* critical reception and, 40–42. *See also* gaze; gender; LGBT film; queering
Shary, Timothy, 77
Show Me Love (*Fucking Åmål*, 1998): awards, 3, 32, 36, 88; casting, 21, 65–66; critical and public reception, 3–4, 36, 40–42, 49, 87–88, 148–49n14;

distribution, 17, 35–36, 40, 49, 119; DVD release, 49; financing and box office receipts, 35, 90, 115; international reception of, 87–89; journal writing technique in, 32–33; lighting, 50, 56–58, 72–73; place/locality as component, 22–23, 65–67, 72–73; plot synopsis, 34–35, 43–45; production history, 86–87; promotional material for, 38–40, 39–40; screenings, 3–4, 68–69, 88; script/dialogue, 14–15, 53; soundtrack, 37, 45, 68, 72; title of, 36–38, 90–91
The Silence (*Tystnaden*, Ingmar Bergman, 1963), 26, 54, 58–62
Sir Arne's Treasure (*Herr Arnes pengar*, Mauritz Stiller, 1919), 93
Sixteen Candles (John Hughes, 1984), 77
Sjöström, Victor, 26, 27, 74, 93
social realism, 27, 54, 84–85, 151n40
Soila, Tytti, 165–66n81
Some Kind of Wonderful (John Hughes, 1987), 77
Sonet Film, 36, 40
soundtracks: Dogme 95 guidelines for, 47; image-soundtrack disconnect in *Container*, 7; pop music in *Show Me Love*, 37, 45
spatial ambivalence, 9, 91–92, 98, 112
Srinikornchot, Run, 21
Steene, Birgitta, 96
Steinberg, Mark, 131
Stiller, Mauritz, 26, 73–74, 93
Strand, Lina, 50, 100
Strandlind, Kalle, 17, 104
Street, Sarah, 112
Summer with Monika (*Sommaren med Monika*, Ingmar Bergman, 1953), 74, 94
Svensk filmindustri, 113–14, 119
Svensk Television (SvT), 16–17
Svensson, Maria, 100
Sweden. *See* class; national identity; Swedish film
Swedish film: adolescence/childhood as theme in, 5, 53, 89–90; authenticity as concern in, 8–9; decentralization of, 84, 87, 105, 108, 113, 118; European Union regionalization initiative and, 106–11, 121–22; Film Production and Distribution Treaty of 1963, 112–14; landscape as common feature in, 92–93; male protagonists in, 21; Memfis Film role in, 16–17, 116–18; outsider films, 105; sexuality in, 73–74, 90; *Show Me Love* criti-

cal reception, 40–42; *Show Me Love* references to Swedish film history, 32; small town settings in, 84, 86, 92, 96–97, 100–101, 113; social realism as theme in, 27, 54, 84–85, 151n40; Swedish national cinema, 86–87, 112–14, 165–66n81; transnational film and, 112–16; U.S. influence in, 87

Swedish Film Institute, 16, 36, 107, 113–14

Swedish welfare state, 26–27, 80, 93–96, 102, 124–27

Södergran, Edith, 62

Talk (*Bara prata lite*, 1997): Brantås as cinematographer for, 48; cinematography for, 18; as Jönsson collaboration, 14; sisterhood in, 59

Tarkovsky, Andrei, 6

teen movie genre, 76–77, 90–91

Three Strange Loves (*Törst*, Ingmar Bergman, 1949), 26

Through a Glass Darkly (*Såsom i en spegel*, Ingmar Bergman, 1961), 26–27, 95

Thunberg, Karin, 41

Timm, Mikael, 117

Titanic (James Cameron, 1997), 90

Together (*Tillsammans*, 2000): overview, 123–27; awards, 168n2; Brantås as cinematographer for, 48; casting, 67; cinematography, 18, 51; distribution, 17, 168n2; filming location, 22–23, 25, 103–4, 109; financing and box office receipts, 4, 168n2; Moodysson ambivalence about, 12; production design, 7, 125; script revision process, 14–15; teenagers as theme of, 5; welfare state as them in, 26–27, 124–27

Toronto Film Festival, 88

translations (of films), 20

transnational film, 23–24, 98, 112–17, 129, 133–34, 134–35

Trier, Lars von: critique of Christian tragedy, 130; delocalization strategies in, 97–98, 160n35; Dogme 95 affiliation, 24–26, 46, 94–95; Moodysson parallels with, 24–26; as Trollhättan filmmaker, 97–98, 111, 160n35; as Zentropa co-founder, 118

Troell, Jan, 27, 54, 96, 115–16

Trollhättan, Sweden (Moodysson filming location): economic status of, 101–2, 120–21; European Union regionalization initiative and, 106–7, 163n53; importance to Moodysson, 23,

25–26, 95–96; local involvement in *Show Me Love*, 66–67, 72–73; location substitution and, 34, 99–103; outsider status of, 105; *Show Me Love* significance for, 147n5; as "Trollywood" production center, 86, 103, 105, 109; as von Trier location, 25–26, 97–98, 111, 160n35
Truffaut, François, 52–53
Trust Film Sales, 17, 119

Unwerth, Ellen von, 49
Uppgörelse i den undre världen, en (*Settlement in the Underworld*, Dramatiska Institutet exam film), 14
U.S. film industry: European regionalism compared to, 112; heteronormative gaze as feature of, 28–29, *30–31*; high school films, 76–77, 81, 89–90; Hollywood Production Code, 75; Hollywood themes in *Show Me Love*, 31–32; *House of Angels* success, 118; influence in Swedish film, 87; as Moodysson influence, 12, 78; Moodysson U.S. production proposal, 132; sexuality in U.S.-distributed Swedish films, 42, 73–74; *Show Me Love* promotion/reception, 37, 38, 39, 43

Vacker sjuk plats, En (A Beautiful Sick Place, autobiographical report, 2012), 5
Van Sant, Gus, 74
vegetarianism, 11, 65
Verhoeven, Paul, 75
verisimilitude, 27, 85
Vinterberg, Thomas, 24, 46, 47, 94–95
voice-over, 32–33

Walk on the Wild Side, A (Edward Dmytryk, 1962), 75
Wanner, Catherine, 131
Widding, Astrid Söderbergh, 165–66n81
Widerberg, Bo, 6, 27, 54, 151n40
Wings (*Vingarne*, Mauritz Stiller, 1916), 73–74
Winter Light (*Nattvardsgästerna*, Ingmar Bergman, 1963), 95

Zentropa, 16–17, 111, 115, 117–18
Zetterling, Mai, 27
Zorn, Anders, 93
Zyskind, Marcel, 24, 136